Endorsements

of

Little Mo's Legacy: A Mother's Lessons, A Daughter's Story

"In the early years of my tennis career, I was compared to Little Mo. I always took it as a compliment, but it wasn't until I read Cindy's book that I truly understood the greatness of Maureen Connolly and how flattering that comparison really was. I only hope that now the comparison extends to my role as wife and mother. I loved the stories in the book and found them to be very inspiring. Thank you, Cindy, for telling us more about your mother and for giving us all the lovely gift of *Little Mo's Legacy*." —**Tracy Austin, Youngest Winner of US Open, and Former #1 Women's Tennis Player in the World**

"Cindy's telling of her mother's legacy is wonderfully personal and affirmative. In language that echoes the words exchanged between the immortal Mo Connolly and a daughter who was the best of learners, Mo Connolly's intensity, human spirit, and abiding influence unfold. The book is true, joyful, and triumphant." —**John T. Casteen III, President University of Virginia**

"Cindy's book is a loving tribute to her mother, a legend in the tennis world. The lessons she learned in the few short years with her mother are wonderful guidelines for parents as how to rear a Godly, loving, caring, and responsible child. It is a well-written, heartwarming book showing a daughter's intense love of her mother and a great tribute to her memory." —**Kenneth H. Cooper, M.D., M.P.H., Cooper Clinic**

"Compassion for others is not a genetically inherited trait. It is one that is taught to us by a loving momma and daddy. Cindy's mother taught her well. *Little Mo's Legacy* inspires us as we see a young girl's positive spirit turn the grief of her mother's death into action. This book will tenderly touch your life." —**George D. Farr, President & CEO, Children's Medical Center of Dallas**

"Through Cindy's eyes, those of us who never knew Maureen Connolly Brinker see her enormous legacy of love and courage. This book is an inspiration." —**Kay Bailey Hutchison, U.S. Senator**

"I was fifteen years old when I had the thrill of first meeting Maureen. Over the years, our paths crossed many times. She was a total inspiration and role model to me. *Little Mo's Legacy* outlines the principles that made a champion on and off the court. It is a remarkable book for all ages." —**Billie Jean King, Winner of 20 Wimbledon Titles, Named by** *Life Magazine* **as one of the 100 Most Important Americans of the 20th Century, and Cofounder, World Team Tennis**

"Little Mo was a champion at tennis. Had her accident not cut short her remarkable career, we all would have been chasing her records. More importantly, she was a champion at life by affecting others in such a positive way. Everyone who follows the lessons that Maureen taught Cindy is a winner." —**Martina Navratilova, Winner of 56 Grand Slam Titles, Member of International Hall of Fame, and Aspiring Philanthropist**

"Maureen, 'Little Mo,' Connolly was one of the greatest women's tennis players of all time, receiving many honors throughout the world. Through *Little Mo's Legacy*, we now know she was an even greater mother and wife. This touching book is the finest honor Maureen and Cindy's father, Norman, will ever receive. Cindy inspires us with the invaluable lessons she learned from a world champion mother, Little Mo. I couldn't put this book down!" —**Ross Perot, Founder, Perot Companies**

"Being a world-class athlete takes discipline, determination, and dedication. Little Mo was gifted with these tremendous attributes. But more importantly, she shared her skill of living with her daughters, Cindy and Brenda. The inspiring lessons in *Little Mo's Legacy* could change your life. They certainly will bless it!" —**Roger Staubach, Professional Football Hall of Fame, Chairman & CEO, The Staubach Company**

"Little Mo and I warmed up together before we each won the French championships at Roland Garros in 1954. She played with supreme confidence and determination and possessed a very strong will to win. She was a terrific champion and a better human being. Cindy does a beautiful job of describing what a wonderful wife and mother she was as well. I'll bet you won't be able to finish reading *Little Mo's Legacy* without shedding a tear. I couldn't!" —**Tony Trabert, Winner of 5 Grand Slam Singles and Doubles Titles, Member International Tennis Hall of Fame**

Little Mo's Legacy

A Mother's Lessons
A Daughter's Story

by

Cindy Brinker Simmons

with

Robert Darden

TAPESTRY PRESS
Irving, Texas

Tapestry Press
3649 Conflans Road
Suite 103
Irving, Texas 75061

Printed in the United States of America

05 04 03 02 01   5 4 3 2 1

Library of Congress Cataloging-in-Publication Data

Simmons, Cindy Brinker, 1957-
  Little Mo's legacy : a mother's lessons, a daughter's story / by Cindy
Brinker Simmons with Robert Darden.
      p. cm.
  ISBN 1-930819-01-3 (alk. paper)
  1. Connolly, Maureen, 1934-1969. 2. Tennis players—United
States—Biography. 3. Women tennis players—United States—Biography.
4. Women tennis players—United States—Family relationships. 5.
Simmons, Cindy Brinker, 1957- I. Darden, Bob, 1954- II. Title.
  GV994.C64 S56 2001
  796.342'092—dc21

                                    2001001232

Cover, book design, and layout
by D. & F. Scott Publishing, Inc., North Richland Hills, Texas

Dedications

In loving memory of my mother,
Maureen Connolly Brinker, a true champion.

To my dad, Norman, Mom's dearest love
and the joy of his two daughters.

To my sister, Brenda, who shares the blessing
and honor of Mom's legacy with me.

To my husband and best friend, Bob,
my greatest source of love and encouragement.

To my son, William, who loves his Grandma Mo
without ever having met her.

Most importantly, with heartfelt gratitude
to my Lord and Savior Jesus Christ
for blessing my life beyond measure
with this precious family.

—Cindy Brinker Simmons

I would like to dedicate this book
to Rachel Barkley
on the occasion of her baptism
on October 29, 2000. We love you, Rachel.

—Robert Darden

Contents

Acknowledgements

This book began sixteen years ago when I felt the need to chronicle my memories of Mom and the impact she had on my life. In reality, *Little Mo's Legacy: A Mother's Lessons, A Daughter's Story* began when I was born in 1957. As I took my first breath, my mother was by my side, lovingly cuddling her newborn. Throughout my first twelve years, she was always by my side—as a coach, as an encourager, as a proud mother. Following her death in 1969, her lessons took root and grew along with me, enriching my life, even though her physical presence was gone. In some ways, I understand and appreciate her mentoring in greater measure today than I did some thirty years ago.

However, this book is not mine alone. So many people have been part of this story and have influenced the shaping of my life as well as the direction of *Little Mo's Legacy*.

Both Mom and Dad taught me the importance of sharing what I have with others. That's why I wrote this book. They both gave my little sister, Brenda, and me valuable insights into the skill of living through their very example, and I am hopeful that those lessons, captured within these pages, will be very meaningful to all who read them.

I am deeply grateful to Dad for his input in this project. He has always been there for me. My love and respect run deep for this incredible hero in my life.

Brenda has been the only other person to have had the unique privilege of calling Little Mo "Mom." Brenda is an awesome sister, and I have learned so much from her wisdom and maturity over the years. As I wrote this book, I gained even more insight about Brenda from what she shared with me of her experience as a ten-year-old seeking to cope with Mom's death. Dealing with the loss of a mother is painful at any age, and grieving privately is part of the process of healing. Brenda's strength of character, kindness, and courage have always had my highest respect. After this book, my love for her has only grown deeper. I truly cherish her.

May this book also be a source of encouragement to Brenda's husband, Steve, and my adorable niece and nephew, Connolly and Connor. May they both learn more about their Grandma Mo from these pages.

There are not enough words to thank my beloved Bob for his part in this book. He stayed up late hours reviewing copy and even spent two full days in the garage trying to find my diaries—which he did! His support and love inspire me daily. How I give thanks for him in my life!

William, dear one, may you understand as you grow older that it is a privilege to have the legacy that you carry through Grandma Mo. She had a servant's heart and my prayer for you, bright joy in my life, is that giving to others will be continued through many generations to come in our family. What a difference that investing in people's lives makes in your own.

Special, heartfelt thanks go to Nancy Jeffett and Ben Press for their steadfast loyalty and friendship to Mom. You have taught me the value of those precious, lifelong relationships. Mom loved you both so much.

To Meg Adams, Sally Bremond, Paula Hill, Louise Kane, Betty Lovell, Dianne Ogle, Janet Rusche, Suzanne Schutze, Arlene Scott, Markita Thompson, and Dana Williams—my prayer warriors who have lifted up this book and its author—how I thank you. You sustained me and undergirded me in your prayers when I needed them so much.

I am so grateful to my outstanding team at Brinker Communications: Debby Dudley, Camille Grimes, Tiffany Taylor, Sam Bert Jr., Kenna Sloan, and Beth Doolittle. My sabbatical from the office to complete this work of love was seamless because of your tremendous talents. I so appreciate your support.

A business is only as strong as its clients, and I also offer heartfelt thanks to all of our clients who have served as a source of encouragement, cheering me on in this process. That gave me great comfort!

I would also like to acknowledge Stan Levenson, who has had a profound impact on my business success with his support and mentorship.

A special word of thanks to Sandy Halliburton for encouraging me in this project and helping coach me along the way.

I have the privilege of serving on numerous nonprofit boards and am honored to do so. Two of those charities, Wipe Out Kids' Cancer and the Maureen Connolly Brinker Tennis Foundation, will be receiving equal portions of the proceeds from the sale of this book. I founded Wipe Out Kids' Cancer in 1980 in memory of my mother and I want to express my appreciation to our executive director, Paige McDaniel, and our outstanding Board of Directors. Mom and Nancy Jeffett cofounded the Maureen Connolly Brinker Tennis Foundation in 1968. Nancy has taken the torch in Mom's memory and carried it gallantly, building the foundation into one of the largest private tennis foundations of its kind in the world. I want to offer a special thank you to Carol Weyman for her leadership as executive director of the foundation. She has done such great work and has made the foundation flourish with her tremendous talents.

To Pauline and Bill Simmons, two marvelous people who happen to be the greatest in-laws a person could have, I say thanks with all my love. And a big hug goes to one of the dearest people I know—my sister-in-law Katina Simmons. God blessed me when I became an official member of the Simmons family!

To Christina, Chad, Eric, and Mark, I love you. May you find this book meaningful and enjoyable.

Acknowledgements

Alicia Landry gets a very special thank you for her tender foreword to the book. She is such a gracious lady! What a pleasure to know both her and her late husband, Coach Tom Landry. I continue to be touched by the love they radiated to each other and to all who know them.

To Jill Bertolet, president of Tapestry Press, many thanks for your continued enthusiasm for this book and for your friendship. It has meant so much to me.

To Robert Darden, you have been so much fun to work with! Thanks for your help in honoring my memory of Mom. She was such a grand lady and deserves a fine tribute. It was a wonderful experience to do this important book with you.

Finally, I give thanks to God, who has brought such dear and significant people together in my life in such a unique way. He gave me the family I love, the friends I treasure, and the faith that holds it all together. To Him goes all the glory!

Foreword

lthough everyone knew about Maureen "Little Mo" Connolly Brinker, I never actually met her. But I did come close once. When Tommy and I first moved to Dallas with the Cowboys, a local television station called and asked if I could do an interview with them. This was my first interview as a head coach's wife, and I was very nervous.

When I got to the station, I discovered that Maureen had been interviewed just before I was scheduled to go on, but that she had already left. When I went into the studio, the interviewer, a pretty young lady, was in tears. Maureen had just told her that she'd been diagnosed with cancer. In those few short minutes, Maureen had made such a difference in that interviewer's life that she cried when Maureen left.

I *have* known her daughter Cindy for a long while, though I'm not sure how we first met. Perhaps because she has been so active in helping people through organizations like Wipe Out Kids' Cancer or the Maureen Connolly Brinker Tennis Foundation. Or perhaps it was through the Fellowship of Christian Athletes—something my husband was very committed to. Tommy did lots and lots of volunteer work in general—perhaps I met her through him.

It doesn't really matter. What matters is that Cindy Brinker Simmons is a gracious, loving, totally committed Christian woman. She is the most joyous person in the world. I love being around her. Her joy is infectious.

But the reason I'm so delighted to write this foreword to *Little Mo's Legacy* is that Cindy and I share a special bond.

Just as Cindy lost her mother, I lost my precious youngest daughter Lisa Landry-Childress in May 1995, after a four-year battle with liver cancer.

Lisa and her husband Gary had been trying unsuccessfully for years to have a baby. She found out that she was pregnant on the same day she was diagnosed with liver cancer. For her safety, the doctors urged her to end the pregnancy. But Lisa refused. Instead, she prayed that she would live long enough that her daughter would know her. And after Christina was born, Lisa dedicated herself to teaching her everything she could.

Lisa died when Christina was four.

That was five years ago. Today, Christina *does* remember her mother. Every time I'm with her, I see so much of Lisa in her!

Here is just one example. We recently went on a vacation together. One morning, I went in early and found Christina reading a Bible she'd found in a drawer. She said, "Honey (all my grandchildren call me Honey!), I like reading the Bible, especially early in the morning when no one else is up. It comforts me so much."

That's so much like her mother!

And that's why Cindy and I have such a special relationship. During those years, when I worried if Christina would remember her mother, I would see Cindy. And in Cindy, I could see how a mother could make a difference, even in a very young child. It gave me comfort, knowing that Lisa could—and did!—make a difference. Each time I'd see Cindy, and see how great she turned out, I'd realize that Christina probably would, too.

If you have had a great loss in your life, I believe *Little Mo's Legacy* will comfort you. And, if you are one of those fortunate few who have not suffered loss, this story will inspire you.

These are the twin legacies of Maureen Connolly Brinker and Lisa Landry-Childress.

—Alicia Landry

Introduction

I remember my mom. The record books say Maureen Connolly—better known to her adoring fans in the early 1950s as "Little Mo"—was one of the greatest women's tennis players of all time. She won Wimbledon in 1952, 1953, and 1954. In fact, she never lost a singles match the last year of her competitive career. In 1953, she was the first woman—and still the youngest—to have won the Grand Slam of tennis (winning the Australian, French, Wimbledon, and U.S. Open titles in a single calendar year). Only two other women and two men have won the Grand Slam in the history of tennis.

But a serious injury ended her career on July 20, 1954. She was not yet twenty. I was born in 1957 and never saw her play competitively. I didn't even know that she was famous until I was ten years old.

She died when I was 12.

Often, when faced with heartache, tragedy, or trauma, shock sets in. Sometimes you can forget the memories. God does that to preserve and to protect us.

But I remember my mom.

The most striking thing about her was her smile. I think first of her lips and mouth, and then her eyes—always smiling, always flashing. I remember Mom's sparkle.

I remember that she did a host of funny little things. I remember she wore Chanel No. 5 perfume.

There was an aura about Mom—her smell, her laugh, her eyes. Her skin was so beautiful—it was flawless. She was always tan she had brown eyes. And she was always smiling.

Throughout my life, people have told me that Mom wasn't particularly gorgeous or glamorous, but that she had a special radiance about her. She would walk into the room and people would do a double take because of this radiance.

Because it gave me such a sense of security, I especially remember my mom and dad always touching— always touching, always laughing, always together. He called her Mosey. She called him Lovey. One of our homes in Dallas had a split-level living room. In the upper living room, we had a few chairs, several sofas, and one big old leather chair that was Dad's. So many times I saw my dad sit down in his chair and seconds later Mom would just plop in his lap. Only one chair would do for her—it was the chair that he was in. The love between them was so strong that it gave my little sister Brenda and me a great security in life. Other people sensed it, too. They loved to congregate in our home because of that feeling of love and inclusiveness. I still have people tell me that Mom's and Dad's relationship affected them deeply.

We also had a number of promising junior tennis players who came and stayed at our house for an entire school year so that Mom could coach them in tennis. She wanted to share the sport she loved so much with young players. Of course, I loved it—I had always wanted an older sibling. We would go to the tennis courts and I'd sit on the sidelines and watch them play—my mom and my new big sisters. Some of the players on the women's professional circuit would also come to our house when they had a week off. Mom would coach them, but it wasn't just the tennis that drew them to Dallas. They always felt special at the Brinkers' home.

We had great meals at the dinner table. Mom loved to cook. Dinner times were when we all came together. My mom's mother, whom Brenda and I called Nana, also lived with us. Nana did a lot of the cooking, too. No phones were answered. No business was conducted during dinner hours. No interruptions were tolerated; family time was always sacred. Our dinner table served a smorgasbord of family discussions, vacation planning sessions, and personal strategy meetings.

My mom wasn't pretentious; she was a real person. She usually wore sweatpants and never had any scrapbooks of her meteoric career around the house. At night, we sat around the fireplace and talked. Mom would always ask, "How was your day at school?" We didn't talk about tennis. She avoided that topic because she didn't want us to feel the pressure of following in the footsteps of a famous parent.

When I was ten, I went to a tennis camp in Carmel, California. This was a time in my life when it wasn't very cool to have your mom around. But on the final day of camp, Mom was invited to speak. I couldn't understand why. I was at the camp with the daughter of actor Tony Curtis and his wife, actress Janet Leigh. The camp director hadn't asked either one of them to speak. Why my mom? She wasn't famous, was she? I just didn't get it. In fact, I was a bit embarrassed. My mom had never told Brenda and me about her fame and celebrity. So I was the last among my friends to learn that I had a famous mother.

Mom was sick for two years when I was ten and eleven, but she still did everything. She was the room mother and went on school trips with us. She was always there for us.

And that's the way she was to the end.

This is the story of my mom and the lessons she taught me.

This is the story of the lessons she taught me in life and in death.

This is the story of Maureen Connolly Brinker.

I'm her daughter Cindy.

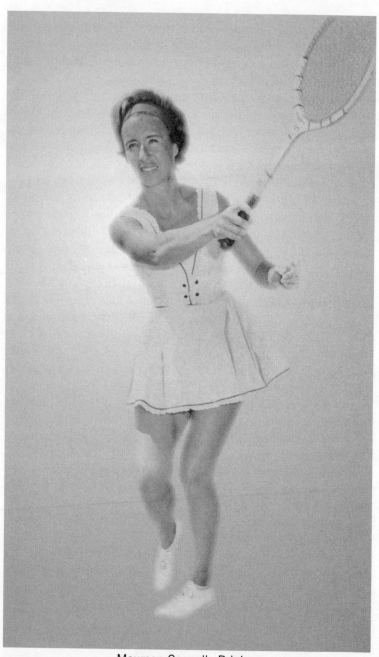

Maureen Connolly Brinker

Little Mo's Legacy

Little Mo as Little Mom

"I've lived ten lives."
—Maureen Connolly Brinker

She was the typical mom. She was always there for me, with school, with tennis, with life. Mom had wanted to be a mother so much. She was reared a Catholic and what she wanted most in life was to have children.

In 1957, Mom wrote a book, *Forehand Drive* (now out of print). After recounting her fabulous career, she ended with this charming epilogue:

> This book should have an ending. My career certainly did. But now, there is to be a beginning, and my thoughts are in the centre court of Babyland. We are to have a baby in 1957. A tennis champion? A great horseman? We have ordered neither a special racket nor a riding crop. Our baby will have just a plain ordinary rattle.

> There will be no prompting in the wings as our child grows up. He'll be exposed to tennis, riding and other sports, but he won't be forced along any championship trail. If he loves tennis, that's fine; he'll get plenty of help from Mother. But if his interest lies in rocket-ship trips to the moon, with a shuttle-run to Mars, we'll sit on the sidelines and cheer.

> To me, my career was glorious. I would be happy to have
> a young tennis star in the family, but the burning fire to
> be the best—at anything—must come from him alone.
>
> All we want is a normal, happy youngster, and we'll let
> him follow his own star in his own way.

Imagine their surprise when their budding rocket scientist/tennis star turned out to be a *she* instead of a *he!*

On the day I was born, it was chronicled around the world that Maureen Connolly Brinker had given birth to another "Little Mo." One newspaper article began, "Norman and Maureen are so excited about the birth of their new daughter, Cynthia Ann." But the final quote from Mom in the story read, "Well, maybe next time it'll be a boy." Mom desperately wanted to have a boy for Dad since he was the only male Brinker. But it was never meant to be.

On the other hand, Mom got the "normal, happy youngster" she wished for in her epilogue. I had an idyllic childhood, surrounded by loving, supportive parents.

Mom repeatedly told reporters that she'd never been happier than when playing the role of wife and mother. She stored her three hundred trophies in a backyard storeroom and threw herself into the role of parent with the same fervor with which she'd driven herself on the clay courts of the U.S. Open and the grass courts of Wimbledon.

"Certainly it was wonderful," she once told reporter Eugenie Sedlock, "playing the big matches— and winning. But you're under such pressure. You don't have time to enjoy your triumphs because of that pressure. You're constantly pushing to do better and win more because that's what's expected of you.

"Now I'm under no pressure. Taking care of Cindy is fun and I love it!"

Still, she admitted to Sedlock that motherhood was a full-time job:

"Busy is an understatement. I take care of Cindy, cook, launder, and iron. I have a cleaning woman once a week because I hate to clean. Anyway, dust gives me hay fever. Three afternoons a week I give tennis lessons. Keeps me in trim and close to tennis which, of course, I'll always love. My mother, Jessamine Connolly, baby-sits when I'm away."

In addition to the lessons, Mom wrote for various newspapers (including *The London Daily Mail*) and lectured on behalf of a sporting goods firm that manufactured Maureen Connolly autographed rackets.

"I intend to keep Cindy first, though. I want nothing to cheat me out of her babyhood. And Norm agrees with me completely."

Mom then proceeded to tell Eugenie in minute (and embarrassing!) detail every aspect of my life, down to my burping and passion for strained peas—all of which ended up in the newspaper. Even at the tender age of four months, Mom was already thinking of my future, declaring that I wouldn't follow in her footsteps unless I wanted to.

"We want her to express herself in whatever way she chooses. What I'd really like is for her to be a dancer. Whatever she is, I hope she'll excel in it.

"I'm just old-fashioned, I guess, but Cindy is going to be brought up the way I was. If she needs a spanking when she's older, she'll get it.

"Meanwhile, I'm learning with her. She's so bright and alert and healthy."

Spoken like a true proud parent! And she kept her word on the occasional (and probably well-deserved) spankings!

I was born three years after Mom's incredible tennis career was brought to an end prematurely by a riding accident that limited her ability to run. Consequently, I never saw her play in her prime. But I did watch her play tennis in clinics, lessons, and charity events. She was still good. She was remarkable, actually, even though her right leg kept her from running after the ball like she had during her days as a champion.

She loved teaching lessons and giving clinics because it was her way of working. She was very much a working mom. Even when she gave lessons, she would take Brenda and me along because she liked to always have us with her. I loved to watch her pulverize the ball.

Mom was only about five feet four inches tall, but she was all muscle. Even when I saw her play, she still had a strong groundstroke game. She played with a steel racket, a T-2000, and she was not a volleyer. She had a one-handed backhand.

There have been all kinds of sports surveys through the years on who were the best athletes of all time. Mom was voted "Woman Athlete of the Year" by the Associated Press three consecutive years. Many of the top sports writers who saw Mom play in the 1950s think she would have beaten today's stars. She was a power player. Her ground strokes were so precise that she could have passed most of them at the net, then out-rallied them on the baselines.

She would hit the lines of the court twenty to thirty times during each set. It is very difficult for anyone to beat someone with that level of accuracy. Her timing and coordination were absolutely incredible.

Probably the man who knew her tennis game best was her lifelong friend (and an outstanding tennis player himself), Ben Press. Ben saw Mom play at her peak. They continued to play exhibitions in San Diego long after she'd retired. And because he's still active in tennis, he's seen most of today's greatest players as well. A reporter once asked Ben how Mom compared.

"My son and Cindy are almost exactly the same age," he said. "Whenever a Venus Williams or someone comes into the public eye, my son always kids me by saying, 'Well, she's good. But she's no Maureen Connolly, is she?'

"Over the years I've seen them all and, in my opinion, she's still the best player of all time. Obviously she was the best player of her era. No one has come close to all those wins in such a short amount of time."

Her career was truly breathtaking. She is ranked seventh in the history of women's tennis for total Grand Slam singles titles won. What is amazing is that she only competed in the Grand Slam tournaments for three years. The other top six female players ahead of her in this ranking had careers that spanned ten to sixteen years!

Some of today's commentators think Venus Williams could have beaten Mom with her power and speed. Not Ben:

> Here's how I know: I once booked an exhibition at Golden Hall in San Diego. I had Maureen playing Nancy Kiner, who was a well-known tennis player of the day, while Pancho Gonzales played Pancho Segura. Both Maureen and Pancho Gonzales won.
>
> Then I had them play mixed doubles, with Segura playing with Mo. We played on boards that day—which is the fastest possible surface for playing tennis. It's like serving on glass. At the time, Pancho Gonzales had the best serve in the world—it was easily the fastest. Maureen insisted that he not hold back. And yet, she handled Pancho's serve beautifully every time. *Every time.*
>
> As fast as Venus Williams's serve is, it isn't as fast as Pancho Gonzales's. And even if Venus moved faster, I believe that Maureen had better footwork.
>
> And when she played, she had the most uncanny concentration I have ever seen.

On the court, Mom was very focused and intent. In fact, she was sometimes called "Little Miss Poker Face." She was very stoic, very much in control. It was something she'd learned very young.

Mom was raised by a single mother in San Diego. Her father was a lieutenant commander in the U.S. Navy, but her parents divorced when she was only four years old. A few years later, Mom and Nana received word that Mom's father had died in an automobile accident in Texas. Years later, they discovered the error of this report when Mom's father contacted her after her career-ending accident. Mom and her father enjoyed a close relationship throughout the rest

of her life. Still, during her childhood, there was practically
no money, and she learned early on to work hard to overcome obstacles and accomplish her goals.

As a youngster of nine, Mom hung around the tennis
courts two doors from her home until a local tennis pro,
Wilbur Folsom, gave her free lessons in exchange for shagging balls. He saw right away that Mom had unbelievable
hand-eye coordination.

Ben said he only saw one other athlete who equaled
Mom's hand-eye coordination. By a strange coincidence, it
belonged to another young athlete who grew up in Mom's
neighborhood. His name was Ted Williams—and he's in the
Baseball Hall of Fame in Cooperstown as the greatest hitter
who ever lived. There must have been something in that
neighborhood's water!

Ben said that even at a young age, Mom already had that
extra-special something that separates good players from
champions—an eagerness to learn and an intensity to excel.

"Any championship career has foundation stones," Mom
wrote in *Forehand Drive*. "Mine was slavish work and driving
determination. Even at the outset, Folsom became aware of my
burning inner fire because, either in pity or compassion, he vol-
unteered to give me a few pointers. In return, I would become
his ball boy."

And when Mom wrote "driving determination," she was
serious. In the 1940s, there was a stigma attached to being
left-handed. Mom was left-handed. When Folsom casually
mentioned to Mom that most top tournament players were
right-handed, she made the difficult switch without hesitation.

In *Forehand Drive*, she wrote, "By the time I was ten I
had a goal and that was to be the best in the world."

She wasn't kidding.

Folsom's protégée quickly began to catch people's attention. Mary Hardwicke Hare, the British women's champion
and second-ranked woman in the world in the late 1930s,
recalls their first meeting when Mom was eleven. Mary was

touring the United States at that time, conducting tennis clinics, and San Diego was one of her stops:

"Wilbur Folsom had set up that I would hit with Maureen, who was not known as Little Mo then, during her lunch hour at school. As we played, I could see she was totally formed in her stroke production, which was unusual at that age. After the hour, she excused herself to get back to school, shook my hand, and in one breath she very quickly said, 'Thank you very much. I enjoyed it very much. One day I'm going to be the world's greatest tennis player.' I wondered when I was going to see her again but I *knew* she was going to be a champion because she was so dedicated."

By the time Mom was eleven, she was winning 13-and-under tournaments. At the annual Harper Ink Tournament in San Diego, the late *San Diego Union* sportswriter Nelson Fisher saw Mom demolish her older (and more polished) opponent, 6–0, 6–1. Fisher wrote a column about Mom, dubbing her "Little Mo"—recalling "Big Mo," the U.S.S. Missouri, the battleship that pounded the enemy in World War II. The name stuck, and Mom and Nelson and Sophie Fisher stayed fast friends throughout their lives.

Later, Mom began to work with Eleanor "Teach" Tennant, one of the country's best-known tennis coaches. Teach coached many of the tennis greats of that era, including Bobby Riggs and Alice Marble. On weekends, Mom stayed with Teach in Los Angeles where Teach coached her and worked on her game.

At one point, Teach said of Mom, "She had the ability to assimilate what was taught and to execute it properly. She practiced and practiced and she had no mental blocks or resistance to rigid training. I never once heard her say, 'I can't do that.'"

However, a few weeks after winning her third straight Wimbledon championship in July 1954, a riding accident changed everything. The accident nearly severed the muscles of her right leg below the knee. If a nurse hadn't been at the scene and applied a tourniquet, Mom might have bled to death on the spot. As it was, she carried a wicked scar on her leg for the rest of her life.

One of the most remarkable things about my mom is that she was never bitter about the abrupt end to her competitive tennis career. In fact, her personality was so delightful that people loved to be around her. She still enjoyed playing tennis and when she played, she would always laugh. She had a sweet, melodious laugh. It wasn't husky, but it wasn't a giggle either—it was infectious. She would poke fun at herself if she missed a shot. She didn't do any of that when she played competitive tennis—only when she was having fun in the post-competitive years.

Mom never did anything with less than full gusto. She saw and did and participated. In everything she did, she gave her all, but she always seemed to be enjoying herself at the same time. Perhaps it was her fierce love of life that made her memorable to so many people—including two adoring daughters.

After a rigorous teaching session or a rousing game of tennis, she rewarded herself with her favorite drink. It was a combination of grape juice and 7-Up. Brenda and I loved Mom's special drink. Even to this day, I combine 7-Up or Sprite with most of my juice drinks.

While Mom was enjoying her teaching career, Dad started the Steak & Ale restaurant chain in January 1966. In the early days of Steak & Ale, we would have company parties in our backyard. We always had a live band at these annual parties. Dad would invite his executives and managers and their spouses or dates. The party would end up with everybody in the pool—either voluntarily or involuntarily. The next day, Brenda and I would search the pool for combs and pins and jewelry.

One year at the party we had a band and it was really cranking up about 10:30 p.m. The doorbell rang and a policeman at the door said, "Mrs. Brinker, I don't like to have to tell you this, but I've gotten some calls from the neighbors and you really need to hold the music down."

Mom was just appalled. She said, "Oh officer, I'm so sorry. I'll tell Norman right this minute." She went back and said, "Norman, there's a policeman at the front door and the neighbors have been calling. Please tell the band to ease up."

Dad said, "Okay honey, we'll take care of it."

About an hour later, the doorbell rang again. Mom and I went to answer the door and the same policeman was there.

"Uh, Mrs. Brinker, I'm so sorry, but we're still getting calls from the neighbors. You're just going to *have* to do something about that band."

Mom was mortified. "Oh, I told Norman to turn it down. Officer, I promise you, we'll take care of this immediately."

She found my dad, pulled him aside and said, "Norman, Norman, the policeman was here again. We've just got to knock off a few decibels."

So Dad said, "Okay honey, okay. TURN IT DOWN, GUYS!"

But about 12:30, the doorbell rang, *again*. Mom and I went to the door, and this time she was nearly in tears. The whole way to the door she muttered, "Oh no, oh no." It was the same policeman. But he wasn't dressed in his police uniform—he was wearing civilian clothes.

"Um, Mrs. Brinker, I'm off-duty now and I was wondering . . . could I come in and join the party?"

That was the story of our family's life—everybody wanted to be at our home because we had such fun—and other people sensed it.

Mom grew up Catholic and once even had an audience with the Pope. But she disconnected from the Catholic faith in her late twenties. She had trouble with the ritual aspects of it. Still, Mom and Dad knew that we should go to church, so

Brenda and I went to Sunday school at Spring Valley United Methodist Church in Dallas. When we moved to a different home in Dallas, we attended Northridge Presbyterian. In time, only Brenda ended up going regularly. I dropped out. It wasn't for me back then; I even ridiculed Brenda a little bit for going.

Our other big family activity was horseback riding. We've had more than our share of heartache because of accidents with horses, yet we've always loved them.

It was, as I said, a horse-riding accident that ended what was perhaps the most promising career in the history of women's tennis. After winning her first Wimbledon victory at age seventeen, the citizens of San Diego gave Mom a big, beautiful Tennessee Walker, Colonel Merry Boy. Oh, she loved that horse. But one day Colonel Merry Boy and a cement truck were involved in an ugly collision. Mom's right leg was crushed and all of her calf muscles were severed. She would never play competitive tennis again, but her first words after her surgery were, "How is Colonel?"

At the same time, she never allowed the accident to cool her love of horses. As soon as she was able, she was riding Colonel Merry Boy again. It was important to her that she ride again.

Horses were my dad's first passion as well. He was a member of the 1952 Olympic Equestrian team. In 1954, he was competing in the Modern Pentathlon and had a serious accident during the riding component of that five-part event—had it not been for that accident, he was expected to finish near the top. Then, in 1993, he had a near-fatal accident during a polo match that made national headlines.

Brenda and I weren't immune from our share of accidents either.

One day in Phoenix when I was six, my dad halter-led my horse down the alley on our block. (We had a stable behind our home.) Hilda, our German Shepherd, tagged along. Dad was riding his horse with a saddle and I was riding bareback as we walked along. We stopped to visit with a painter working on a house down the street. Suddenly, Hilda shot out of the bushes chasing another dog. Both the dogs and the horses got excited and one of the dogs bit my horse on the fetlock. The horse bucked, I fell on the cement, and the horse's hoof crashed down on my face. It was not a pretty picture: blood everywhere, a frantic Dad, dogs barking. Dad ran home with me in his arms and called an ambulance. Then, on the way to the hospital, my ambulance crashed into another car. I finally did get to the hospital. I had to have plastic surgery—this is not my original nose!—and I still have a scar on my lip. If the injury had been any higher, I could have been blinded.

Brenda was an accomplished rider. She competed in Mexico City in 1977 as a member of the U.S. Junior Equestrian team, but she had broken several bones from riding along the way. She was once in a body cast for three months. The day after she got out of her body cast, she fell down the stairs and broke her ankle in three places. When we Brinkers fall, we fall hard!

Still, through it all, one big family thing that we did in Dallas was ride horses together. We had a stable behind our home in Dallas and we went for rides around White Rock Lake as a family.

Mom used to say, "I love having the wind in my face. There's nothing better than a good gallop and the wind in your face." Horses were her first love.

Though I occasionally ride today, I always feel a little uncomfortable. But not Mom. She never lost her passion for riding.

Mom was sensitive, yet she was so disciplined. Her life had been such a regimen of discipline that she did not like to deviate from that discipline. Of course, that outlook was always a challenge for a couple of mischievous sisters. I would ask her, "Mom, can I have someone spend the night?"

"No, dear. It's a school night."

Then I'd go to my dad and ask the same thing.

He'd say, "Sure, Cindy."

Mom tried to run a tight ship. For all her various responsibilities and professional commitments, she never wanted to be away from home for more than a night or two.

There would come a time when she couldn't leave at all.

I didn't express much interest in tennis until about the age of ten. Once I showed that I was interested, Mom would go out with me and we would hit some balls as long as I wanted to. One day I was favoring a western grip, which makes you hit the ball wrong. I was comfortable with it and, besides, the ball was going over the net.

Finally, Mom showed me the right way to hold a racket. The result, of course, was that I couldn't hit anything because that new grip seemed unnatural.

I said, "Mom, I think I'll go back to my old way. It works much better." She just smiled.

The next shot, she accidentally hit the ball a little too far from me.

I dropped my racket in disgust and said, "Mom, you're the one who's been playing tennis longer than I have. Surely you can get it a little closer to me. *You're* the one that's supposed to know about this game!"

Afterwards, a friend who had been watching us play walked up.

"Cindy," he said, "do you plan to play tennis as well as your mother?"

I said, "I plan to play much better. Mommy makes too many mistakes to be a good player."

What a nervy little kid!

Mom really didn't teach me. Instead, she thought it would be better to let me take lessons from other people. But she was always there encouraging me. I started playing some

Maureen is all smiles at Wimbledon before a match.

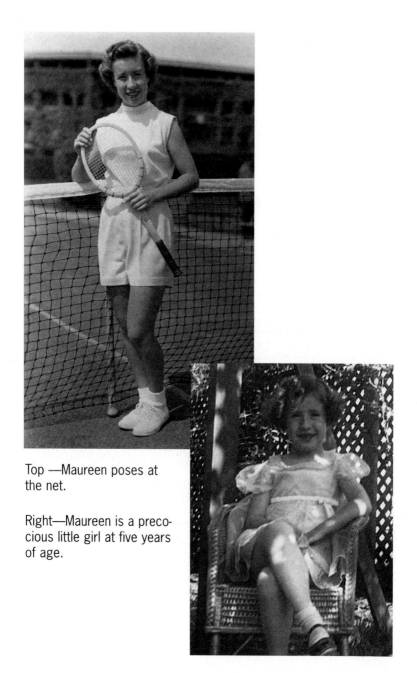

Top —Maureen poses at the net.

Right—Maureen is a precocious little girl at five years of age.

Maureen and her beloved Colonel Merry Boy.

Maureen's smile brightened any rainy day.

Maureen is ready for her next match.

Maureen shares a lively moment with her coach,
Eleanor "Teach" Tennant.

Little Mo in action.

Maureen and Norman married June 11, 1955.

The newlyweds on their honeymoon.

tournaments a year later. One time I won a match that I wasn't supposed to win—actually, I hadn't realized that I *had* won the match at the time. Mom jumped up and down in the stands shouting, "She won, she won, I don't think Cindy knows she won!" I was, of course, both mortified at Mom's enthusiasm and secretly pleased at the same time.

In Dallas, we constantly had tennis players in our home. They ranged from promising junior tennis players who lived with us for a year to pros who would sometimes take a week off the circuit to be with us. Great tennis champions like Ann Hayden Jones and Virginia Wade would stay with us, and Mom would give them coaching tips. Sometimes they would go on vacation with us. How could I *not* grow up to love tennis?

Dad describes Mom as a truly remarkable person who just happened to be a great tennis player. And the other thing he always says is that she was so quietly humble it took his breath away.

How humble? I was the last to know she was famous. It took a little know-it-all kid down the street to clue me in one day when we were playing at my house.

My little friend Sylvia said, "Cindy, you know your mom is famous, right?"

I said, "Sylvia, you've got the wrong mother."

And Sylvia said—very smugly, I might add—"Well, my dad told me that your mom was famous, and my dad doesn't lie."

Surely there was some mistake. At home, there were no scrapbooks laying on coffee tables, no faded newspaper articles on display and no personally autographed celebrity glossy photographs (at least none that I recognized).

Instead, we had a two-toned station wagon, posed school pictures of Brenda and me unsuitable for framing but framed and hung anyway and a year's supply of *National Geographic* stacked neatly next to the bowling trophy. A typical household. Mom might have been perfect, yes, but famous—*never!*

If it was coming from Sylvia, I didn't give it much credence. But the fact that she referenced her dad changed everything. I thought, "Oh my gosh, I better check this out." And so I did.

It was like, for a mother, when you have to tell your child that Santa isn't real and, by the way, it isn't exactly the Easter Bunny who is delivering those eggs. And you don't even *want* to guess the tooth fairy's real identity!

I know now that this conversation must have been difficult for Mom. All of a sudden, her little girl comprehended a different reality. As a mother, you want to hold on to that innocence. Mom had purposely not shared her celebrity status with Brenda and me. We thought that the Wimbledon trophies were just fancy decorations. And we weren't really sure what being "number one" even meant. It was a tough thing for Mom to realize that her little girls were growing up.

Her other secret—that she had cancer—she wasn't quite as ready to reveal.

In January 1967, when I was in fourth grade, we left Dallas for California. The doctors thought the climate might help Mom, but Brenda and I never knew exactly why we went out there—it was just another big adventure for us.

As the cancer spread, Mom wanted to come home to Dallas to die, although it was never mentioned in those words. The only thing I knew was that Dad and Mom were taking a lot more trips to out-of-town hospitals. Something must be wrong. But how wrong? I had no clue.

During the last two years of Mom's life, she would sit us down and talk philosophically. Even though she honestly didn't believe she was going to die, Mom talked a lot about appreciating each moment.

Whenever you're confronted with a potential terminal illness, it makes you appreciate the little things; it makes you appreciate life more. None of us knows when God will call us home.

She'd hug us both and say, "Don't dawdle, honey. Don't waste time. Do what you feel is right and not what other people think. Maximize each day."

I'd smile and say, "Sure, mom," and run out to play.

I didn't know the significance of what she was saying then.

I do now.

When I was eleven, two promising junior tennis players stayed with us so Mom could coach them, Patty Ann Reese and Nancy Ornstein. They were going to live with us the entire school year, so we converted a playroom into a bedroom for them. They went to school in Dallas during the day, and Mom coached them in the afternoons. Mom loved doing it, and I loved having Patty Ann and Nancy as part of our family.

One day, I wandered by their room and saw them packing. That seemed strange to me because they were supposed to be here for the whole year. I went up and said, "Why are you packing? Where are you going?"

They looked at each other but didn't say anything because they knew I didn't know.

Finally, Nancy said, "Well, you might want to go talk to your mom."

I found Mom lying on her bed, resting.

I said, "Mom, are you gonna die?"

She said, "I don't plan to."

I repeatedly asked this same question until the day she died. And I always received the same answer: "I don't plan to."

She didn't want to say *yes* because she really didn't think she was going to die. Even during the worst times, she wouldn't say *yes* because that word had such a finality about it. At the same time, she didn't want to say *no* because she didn't want to build our expectations too high.

So each time I asked, she said, "I don't plan to." And that sufficed.

During this difficult time of her illness, I would have dreams that Mom was sick and dying. They were very disconcerting, very unnerving. I'd get up in the middle of the night, tiptoe into Mom and Dad's bedroom, and I would ask her again, "Mom, are you gonna die?"

And each time she would hug me and say, "Honey, I don't plan to."

It started out as pains in her stomach. By the time the doctors realized it was ovarian cancer, it was too late. But Mom never told us. She never, *ever* told us she was dying.

Today, perhaps, I would do it differently. But this was back in the late 1960s and people didn't talk about such things back then, particularly with their children. So there was never any family discussion, no "Honey, go get the girls. Let's talk about it."

As a result, I never realized her illness was as bad as it was.

Well, perhaps I did once. That memory haunts me to this day.

One afternoon, Mom began screaming in pain. There was a door off of my parent's bathroom that led to their bedroom. It had a little grille in it. When I heard Mom scream, I crept to that grille and sat down on my knees and peered through it. I knew I shouldn't be there, but I just felt so helpless hearing her scream. And I could see her in the bed, writhing in pain.

Dad was with her and must have seen that I was watching. He very quietly came all the way around to where I was. I didn't see him because I was just so transfixed on Mom's pain. All of a sudden, I felt someone putting his strong hands gently over my ears. He kept them there until Mom's pain ebbed enough that she could stand it.

Mom and Dad were Brenda's and my life. We adored the ground Mom walked on. Dad was always this giant of a man. Not because he was big—he was fit and trim, a real athlete—but we felt so protected around him. In that moment, he was protecting me again.

After that, Mom was admitted to Baylor University Medical Center. In the hospital, they would not let children under twelve into the rooms, so Dad had to sneak Brenda and me up to visit.

Still, Mom and Dad never discussed her dying with Brenda and me. I honestly believe it was because Mom, as a champion, wasn't going to let this powerful opponent overcome her. She truly believed she was going to beat it, as if she could will herself well—just as she'd willed herself to victory on the tennis court time and time again.

And after the first surgery, Dad later said they thought they *were* going to beat it. It was ovarian cancer and the doctors had thought—or had hoped—that they'd gotten it all.

But they hadn't.

Even today, ovarian cancer has an appalling death rate. It's not a cancer you can necessarily discover with an annual checkup. Typically, by the time you realize what's happening, ovarian cancer has spread well beyond the ovaries and the survival rate drops to 30 percent and lower when diagnosed at that stage. So when Mom started having those hideous stomach pains, it was far, far too late.

While she still had enough strength, Mom insisted on flying out for three days to the City of Hope Hospital in Duarte, California, to be with Patsy Zellner, her best friend from childhood tennis days and her long-time doubles partner. Patsy was my godmother. She, too, was dying of cancer. Ben Press said that Mom and Patsy were soul mates.

"Maureen's best friend was Patsy Zellner, who at the time was the second best junior in the country," he said. "They went to church together, they practiced together, they went to movies together, they were inseparable.

"Not surprisingly, Maureen and Patsy made it into the finals lots of times. But when Maureen played Patsy, they didn't talk. Instead, Maureen would stare straight ahead and concentrate. And when it was over, even if the final was love and love or love and one, they'd hold hands and walk off together."

Joe Zellner, Patsy's dad, later talked about Mom's last visit with Patsy, just ten days before Patsy died. He said that Mom brought Patsy some of the new blue tennis rackets she was endorsing. She never told Patsy that she had been diagnosed with ovarian cancer. Instead, she'd gone to encourage Patsy.

"This told me what kind of girl Maureen was," he said.

After Mom's cancer was diagnosed, she went to the best doctors in Dallas. When she didn't improve, Mom and Dad went to Memorial Sloan-Kettering Cancer Center in New York for a grueling week-long battery of tests as a last-ditch effort. Was this terminal or not?

At the end of the week, Mom and Dad met with the doctors. Mom knew instantly, looking at the doctors' faces, what the prognosis was.

One of the doctors said, "Maureen, there is nothing we can do here that isn't being done for you in Dallas. There's always a chance, with all of the advances in medicine, that some new treatment may emerge. But with what we know now, I'm afraid, you've had your best days."

After saying that, the doctor had tears in his eyes. He'd been so taken with her, with her courage, with the way she'd responded that week, that he simply broke down.

Dad teared up as well. It was the worst possible prognosis. This was his wife, whom he adored with all of his heart. And now he was going to lose her.

Years later, NBC broadcast a made-for-TV movie about my mom's life, *Little Mo*. In the movie—which was released as a full-length feature film in Japan—two little girls played Brenda and me. The movie ends with a scene where Mom and Dad take us out to the park and tell us that she is going to die.

That never happened. There were none of those discussions in the Brinker household, not even between Mom and Dad.

"We never discussed her disease," Dad once told me. "One day, when she came back from a session with the doctor, I said,

'Mosey, how do you feel? I know what the doctors are saying—but what kind of progress do *you* think you are making?'

"And she said, 'Lovey, the average life expectancy on this disease is three to five years and I've already had two and half.' Boom. That's all she said—but those few words told me how tough she was. Not 'woe-is-me,' not 'why did this have to happen to me?' It was really inspiring for everyone to see how she handled it. Maureen was so positive, that you would have never known she had a problem. You certainly couldn't tell by talking to her.

"That was more than thirty years ago and I'm still in awe of it all. I can't believe how brave she was. She was amazing."

In her final days, Mom came home briefly. I remember how pale, how unnaturally pale, she looked. The sparkle was gone. The smiles were gone. She was barely existing, hanging on through massive infusions of painkillers, blood, and oxygen. When it got too bad, she went back to the hospital for the last time.

On the afternoon of June 21, 1969, Dad was late picking me up from my practice tennis match. I was already feeling tense and irritable. I had turned twelve three weeks earlier and was facing my first year in competitive national tournaments. The 12-and-Under Girls' National Tennis Championships were a little more than a week away in Little Rock, and practicing in the 100-plus degrees of a Dallas summer was a test of endurance.

I wanted to do well for Mom in my very first big national tournament, even if she wasn't going to be able to go with me this time as she had planned.

On the way home after this particularly grueling practice session, Dad's conversation caught my attention. As we neared the site where we'd pick up Brenda that afternoon, Dad's voice dropped to a whisper.

He asked me, "Cindy, what would you do if Mom died?"

The previous few days, she'd looked frailer and weaker than I had ever seen her. Still, this was the first time Dad had talked about *death* or the possibility of it. His intensity frightened me.

"Daddy," I said, "I wouldn't want to live if Mommy didn't."

But he was persistent. "Honey, is that what Mom would want her big girl to say?"

"Well, no, I guess not." I said slowly. "She'd want me to be strong and go on living, even without her. But I wouldn't want to. I really wouldn't want to, you know, Daddy."

"I understand, honey."

Grasping at straws, I stammered, "But it's good that I will never have to live without her because she isn't going to die . . . she just *isn't!*"

My eyes were fastened on Dad's face as he stared ahead over the steering wheel.

"Is she?"

My heart pounded.

Dad turned slowly toward me. But the twinkle and spark and laughter and all the things that made my dad the haven of comfort in every situation were gone.

I was terrified.

"Is she?" I shouted.

"Mom . . ." Dad hesitated. He spoke barely above a whisper. "Mom didn't make it, sweetheart. She tried so hard, but she just didn't make it. Mom died this afternoon."

My dad's voice cracked and for the first time in my twelve years, I saw my hero cry.

2 Growing up without Mom

"The everlasting question is why, in a world which never has enough beautiful people, some of them must leave so soon. We lost another one like that Saturday when Maureen Connolly Brinker died."

—Sam Blair
The Dallas Morning News
June 22, 1969

Mom was thirty-four when she died. Brenda was ten. I was twelve. Mom's funeral service was held at Sparkman-Hillcrest Funeral Home in Dallas. There were television cameras everywhere.

As we were burying Mom, I was keenly aware of those television cameras. "These people are invading our space," I thought. "They shouldn't be here. It's not right." I was angry over the intrusion.

The staring cameras were even more difficult for Brenda. She was embarrassed and grief-stricken and, being a little kid, she didn't really know what to do. So she smiled at the cameras. The next day, the kids at school teased her about smiling at her mother's funeral. It was not what she had meant to do, but when you're invaded like that, with all of the reporters and lights and cameras, it wasn't a place where you felt free to cry, or emote or express what you were feeling.

Sitting at the funeral that day, a resolve suddenly burned within me. It dominated my thoughts. I made a decision right then to do something about the disease that claimed my mom's life so prematurely. With a childlike faith, I asked God to give me an opportunity so that some-day, when I got older, I could crusade against cancer.

When someone you love so dearly dies, the shock creates—at least for a short while—a numbness that makes reality dulled and almost surreal. *How can the people around me laugh and carry on with their lives? How can they go to work, drive in carpools, go to school, enjoy themselves? Can't they see that my world has caved in and fallen apart? Stop, World!*

From my experience, I think that zombie-like state is a way God uses to protect the rawest of emotions that grief produces. It was so hard, at that time, to fully grasp the mag-nitude and impact of losing my mother. She'll never be there to brush my hair, watch my tennis matches, shop for prom dresses, bake cookies, discuss my boyfriends. The loss left me emotionally shattered and empty. Mom, the nucleus of our family, was gone. I couldn't bear the thought of it.

After the funeral service, we went home. Dad grabbed a copy of the daily Dallas newspaper and sat on the side of the bed to read it. I cuddled up next to him. Because she was so admired, there were articles about Mom's death all over the world. And as he started reading story after story, tribute after tribute to Mom, he started to cry again.

I'd always felt my dad was such a protector, such a tower of strength. He was our pillar. I couldn't stand seeing the man who was my hero dissolve in tears.

In the days following Mom's death, even our chocolate poodle, Tallyrand, was affected.

Tallyrand was the coolest dog that ever lived. Tallyrand loved my mom. Whenever Mom came home in her two-tone gold Riviera, Tallyrand would dart over to her side and start jumping up and down. Or, when the car pulled up and Dad was driving, Tallyrand would go to the passenger side and jump up just to get that "Hello, boy" from Mom.

After Mom died, when the Riviera pulled up in the driveway, Tallyrand would routinely run to see her. Each time, with head cocked quizzically, he would peer into the window and realize she wasn't there. I could see his puzzled look. *Where was she?* After a few moments, he would whimper and walk away.

Eventually, he quit coming to the car. He died shortly thereafter. I believe it was of a broken heart. Seeing Tallyrand's confusion and sadness was one of the incidents that forced me to accept the reality that Mom would never come home again.

But what really pounded it into my consciousness was that our house was just dead. The sparkle, the laughter, all those things that make a house a home just weren't there anymore. Dad was great, and he has such a sweet personality. But my mom, as moms are, was the nucleus around which things gravitated in our household. With her passing, the joy was sucked out of the house.

I missed not hearing her voice, not hearing her laugh, not hearing her chat, chat, chat on the phone. The house was deathly silent after that day.

The activities following Mom's death are just a blur now. But a few memories stand out.

For several years, the talented English tennis champion Ann Hayden Jones was consistently in the semifinals of Wimbledon, as well as a number of the Grand Slam tournaments, but she could never win them. She seemed to have a mental block at the major tournaments. Mom worked with her for a number of years on her mental toughness and was one of her closest friends. Whenever Ann had a break from the tour, she would come to our home and Mom would coach her.

In 1969, Mom died on the eve of Wimbledon. For the first time in the tournament's history, the All-England Lawn Tennis Club lowered its flag to half-mast. Ann advanced to the finals that year and won the elusive Wimbledon women's championship. In an interview immediately following her win, she said, "This victory is in honor and memory of my best friend and mentor, Maureen Connolly Brinker." It was such a beautiful tribute—I'll always remember that moment.

The year before she died, Mom cofounded the Maureen Connolly Brinker Tennis Foundation with her dear friend, Nancy Jeffett. When we moved to Dallas in 1963, Nancy contacted Mom and together they decided to help promising young tennis players who couldn't afford lessons or the expenses related to travel—as well as provide an opportunity for people to learn about the sport that Mom and Nancy so dearly loved. Nancy had been a gifted and nationally ranked junior tennis player—reaching a top ten ranking in the United States in the 18-and-under category. The Maureen Connolly Brinker Tennis Foundation eventually was created, and both Mom and Nancy busied themselves on its launching. The first major event for the foundation was to present the Maureen Connolly Brinker Outstanding Junior Girl Award at the 18-and-Under Girls' National Tennis Championships in Philadelphia in 1969. This namesake award would be given to the player at the nationals who best embodied the spirit of Little Mo as a competitor, champion, and good sport. Today, this award remains the most coveted award in junior girls' tennis.

Mom was so excited about this inaugural namesake award and its significance to the fledgling Maureen Connolly Brinker Tennis Foundation. I can remember her practicing and practicing her speech. But she never gave it. Mom died in June. The award was to be presented in August.

Dad, Nancy, and I went to Philadelphia to present the Outstanding Junior Girl Award. A talented young lady named Eliza Pande was the first recipient of the award.

It was all very lovely, but Mom should have been there. She should have been able to give the rousing speech that consumed much of her last pain-wracked months. It was just not fair. It wasn't right. Mom was supposed to be there. But she wasn't. I wanted to be happy, but instead I was grief-stricken.

When the time came to make the presentation, Dad began to speak. But after a few words, he couldn't do it. He became too emotional. So Nancy quickly took his place and, within seconds, she too got choked up and had to stop. Immediately, I went up to the microphone, knees shaking and my heart in my throat. Somehow, I managed to present the award to Eliza.

Slowly, life returned to a somewhat normal pattern. School goes on whether you want it to or not. You've got to practice tennis whether you feel like it or not. You've got to get up in the morning every day, regardless of your emptiness inside.

Mom knew the pressure her daughters would feel following in the footsteps of a famous parent. That's why she discouraged Brenda and me from playing tennis. She was right. The pressure was unbelievable. But I had to fill the emptiness somehow; I chose tennis and my school studies.

Before Mom died, I was, at best, a mediocre student. Mom died in the summer before my seventh grade year. That next year, I was one of only two students that made all As in my graduating seventh grade class. Academics became a harbor of safety for me because I never wanted to deal with Mom's loss. By burying myself in my books, I didn't have to deal with my grief.

Eventually, I graduated third in my high school class.

After Mom died, I grew up. I felt an enormous self-induced responsibility. I realized that I had to get serious. I had to become (or at least I thought I did) the lady of

the house. I don't know if Brenda bought into that concept!
Overnight, there was a dramatic change in my personality.
How I behaved, how I spoke, how I acted changed. I wasn't a
kid anymore.

In 1969, I received a diary for Christmas from my
grandmother (who had kept a diary for fifty-two years!). My
first entry on January 1, 1970 said, ". . . In memoriam to my
understanding mother, I will name you Maureen, dear
diary. Consider it a great honor. Maureen, we are going to
be great friends."

From that point, I addressed each night's entry "Dear
Maureen." I would get in trouble with Dad because I would
frequently stay up till the wee hours of the morning writing.

Sometimes, I would share fun facts with "Maureen" that
I had learned at school. For instance, "It's fascinating to see
how people's dialects differ. Did you know that a frying pan
can be called a spider?" [January 13, 1970]. Other times, I
would share dilemmas, puzzlements and imponderables.
After I made two disappointing grades on two tests in one
day, I wrote that night, "School wasn't very impressive today
. . . all of this, as painful as it is, and getting up at the times I
do for school! . . . Have you ever had homework fever?" [January 20, 1970]. On June 18 of that year, I wrote, "It is drastically hot and humid in Abilene, Mo, and I got a terrible
sunburn. Did you get sunburns when you played tennis?"
And after I won an important tennis match, I wrote, "I am
getting closer to becoming a star like you, Mommy" [February 1, 1970].

Throughout, many entries would end with "Love ya!" or
"Have sweet dreams!"

The entry on June 21, 1970, exactly a year after Mom's
death, bears the still-fresh imprint of her loss on my heart.

> . . . a year ago today, Maureen, you left us on earth. The
> Lord had a reason for it, although it is hard to understand. But you will always remain in our heart and
> minds, and will never really leave us.

Looking back, the diary was my way of communicating with Mom. It was a way for a twelve-year-old who missed her mom to "talk" with her. As my world was changing, I wanted to share my feelings each night with "Maureen."

In the year and a half before Mom died, I had taken an interest in tennis and had started playing some tournaments. However, I really became seriously engaged in the sport after her death. Although I'm not a gifted athlete, I eventually got to be pretty good at it because I practiced so hard. Being competitive and being motivated to accomplish are twin components of my nature—twin legacies of Little Mo. When Mom was alive, tennis had interested me because I was around it so much and it seemed like fun. It was more of a hobby than a passion.

However, after Mom died, I competed in tennis with single-minded fervor and devotion as a tribute to her. I practiced and played hard to keep her memory alive in other's minds—and in my own heart. Tennis kept my love for Mom burning.

As a result, I became a nationally ranked junior. What I lacked in natural ability, I made up in discipline, hard work, and determination.

At one point in the juniors, I consistently beat a young lady who ended up being the world doubles champion for many years. Exasperated, her father came up to me after one match and said, "Cindy, I just don't get it. I don't know how you can beat my daughter because she's so much more talented than you are." I wasn't offended by what he said because I knew it was the truth!

By actively competing on the national junior circuit, I felt that I was carrying on Mom's legacy. And because I was so acutely aware of that legacy, if an opponent's shot would hit close to the line and I wasn't sure if it was in or out, I'd always call it in—against myself. I never wanted Little Mo's daughter to be accused of cheating or hedging. People knew they wouldn't have to get line judges with me—that I was fair beyond reproach. Representing Mom and her legacy became a responsibility that I proudly undertook.

With that single-mindedness, I was the number one ranked junior in Texas in my age division on a consistent basis. I was also one of the top ten or fifteen juniors in the country in my age group throughout my competitive career. But everywhere I went, there was more of a fascination with my being Little Mo's daughter than with my playing abilities and rankings. At important national tournaments around the country, sports reporters would typically interview the top seed. At fourteen, I was ranked tenth in the United States in my age group in singles and fourth in doubles. I had qualified that year to play in the 18-and-Under Girls' National Tennis Championships in Philadelphia. The girls in the tournament were twice my size—I was hardly a threat to the top seeds. However, the first day of the tournament, a huge front page sports article was written about me playing and my chances for a victory. There was no mention of the top seed, or anyone else, for that matter. I was so embarrassed and immediately got trounced in the first round. If you blinked, you might have missed the match! I learned quickly that reporters were not so much interested in my skills, but in the human drama of my bloodline.

However, I believe that sports teaches us much about the game of life and how to compete successfully. Being Little Mo's daughter and playing on her turf taught me how to thrive on pressure and how to be able to meet pressure without succumbing to it. It made me want to work harder. Additionally, competitive tennis became a way to shield myself from the pain of Mom's loss.

While I became absorbed in my tennis and my studies, Dad was the in midst of building a national restaurant chain,

Steak & Ale. After her death, he involved himself in his work as a way of avoiding his pain. He'd lost a lot of momentum with the company because he was with Mom so much those final two years. During Mom's illness, he had devoted virtually all of his time to her—which, of course, is where he wanted to be and needed to be.

I now appreciate and respect Dad's personal priorities with Mom—to the point of his professional sacrifice—so much more than I did as a youngster. His commitment to my mother during those difficult years of her illness has served as an example to Brenda and me.

Brenda dealt with Mom's death in her own personal way. Mom had always called Brenda her "little songbird" because Brenda sang from the moment she got up in the morning to the minute her sweet head sank into the pillow at night. Brenda always had a song in her heart to match the smile on her face. But when Mom died, Brenda quit singing—completely. She grieved privately, as only a sensitive ten-year-old can grieve. Then, in a relatively short period of time, she summoned incredible reserves of strength to adjust to the loss of a mother who was her world.

For me, my healing process was different—and longer. My schoolwork and tennis deflected my pain. Tennis and tennis-related travel kept me from falling into despair. I just didn't want to—I just couldn't—deal directly with the excruciating loss. I was walking with an anesthetized soul. I could never say the word *dead* in reference to Mom. I could never say, "Mom died." Instead, I meticulously used the words *passed away* or other euphemisms.

Still, every night, every single, solitary night in the months following Mom's death, my pillow would be wet because I would cry myself to sleep.

I was never jealous of relationships that girls had with their mothers. Instead, I was happy for my friends who had strong mother-daughter relationships.

But once a group of us were traveling to a tournament and a friend of mine's mother was driving. I was sitting next to my friend in the back seat and all of sudden my friend and her mother got in a little argument. Afterwards, my friend turned to me and whispered, "Cindy, you're so fortunate you don't have a mother. I hate mine."

Her words devastated me. She didn't understand the hurt. Her words were like daggers. She didn't understand she was talking to someone with a hole in her heart. I would have given anything to have a mom, even a mom to argue with—and dislike—at times.

I saw conflict between mothers and daughters, but I ached for it again. I was never resentful of my friends who had really neat relationships with their mothers; I cherished that for them. But over the years, the word "mother" lost its definition for me. On Mother's Day, I never felt a connection. I was sad because of what I knew I was missing on that special day.

After Mom's death, I envisioned the Brinker family as a jigsaw puzzle. Someone had taken that puzzle and thrown it haphazardly to the wind. And we who were left behind had the hard job. We had to reassemble the pieces, make sense of the chaos, and go on.

When Mom passed away, I was not a Christian. But when you lose a parent at an early age, you start asking questions like, "Where is Mom? Is there a heaven? Is there a hell? What's life about anyway?" You get introspective. I wanted some answers.

I was convinced that I had done something terribly, terribly wrong and that this was God's punishment. After all, I was the only kid I knew who didn't have a mom. I really thought that God didn't love me. Or worse, I felt that God was indifferent to me. I believed that God never heard my prayers, much less answered them. I felt like God was very inactive and inconsistent.

In my adolescent mind, I decided that the only way I could earn God's love back was to perform. I felt that the only way I could win anyone's acceptance, affection and approval—particularly the Almighty's—was to perform. And not just to perform, but to perform well.

At Greenhill School, a private school I attended during my high school years, students could choose short elective courses between semesters. I chose a course in religion. I had no clue about religion, but I thought it would be interesting and it might help answer some of the questions I had been struggling with. These electives weren't graded and because I didn't want to do anything that would jeopardize my grade point average, I thought, "Even if I fail it, this is a safe way I can learn a little bit about religion."

The teacher for this elective was Dr. Robert Thornton. I really liked him. But the night before the exam, I did what I typically did in school: I panicked. Fortunately, this was an open book exam, mostly involving faith questions. The answers weren't black and white. Faith statements required some thought and you had to resolve where you were in your spiritual life to answer them. I wasn't *anywhere* spiritually and I knew it.

This test suddenly became very important to me, so I canceled my practice tennis game that afternoon. This was a significant sacrifice for me because at this point in my tennis career, I would practice three hours after school and all day on the weekends. I *never* canceled practice matches, but I canceled this one and drove toward home.

It was here that I reached my "fork in the road" decision. I came to a point where I could either get on the freeway and head home, or stay on the service road and go to my dad's office.

One side of me said, "Cindy, you need to go home and study because you don't have a clue about this exam."

But the other side of me said, "Go to Dad's office."

At the last minute, instead of going home, I decided to go to Dad's office.

He could immediately see that something was up.

"Honey, anything the matter?"

"Oh, no, Dad, everything is fine."

"No, something is the matter."

"Well, I've got this exam and the problem is I know nothing about it. I'm just totally confused. It's religion. It's an open book test tomorrow, but I don't have a clue. I'm really worried. I just wanted to come and tell you I love you and now I'm gonna go home. I just need a hug."

And that's why I went, because I just needed a hug.

But my Dad is a fixer, a problem-solver. Most dads are. It's what makes them happy. He said, "I'll tell you what, Cindy. I've got someone who works for me who is the daughter of a preacher."

"Oh, Dad, she's not in my class. She can't help me."

"Cindy, you just stay here and let me introduce you to her."

"Dad, this is so silly, don't waste your time—or hers. I've got to go home and study."

But it was too late. Mr. Problem Solver had already kicked into action. And there's no stopping Mr. Problem Solver.

"Honey, stay right here."

He called the guy in the office next to him to see if we could borrow his office—which meant some poor employee was kicked out of his own office. Still, out of duty to my dad, I stayed. But I kept wondering, "What could this daughter of a preacher tell me about a class she hadn't taken?"

A little while later, she arrived. My dad introduced me, and we went into this now-vacant office. I think her name was Susan (sadly, I have forgotten the name of this wonderful woman) and she asked me general questions about the course and the exam material. But after a few minutes, she started asking me some thought-provoking questions.

We walked through my life. We talked about my mom's death, about how I felt that God was punishing me, and about how I believed I had to earn God's love.

But Susan told me that I *didn't* have to earn God's love and that, quite candidly, *no one* could earn their way into heaven because we would have to be *perfect* if our entry was based on our own merits. I knew immediately that I couldn't make *that* cut.

We talked about tennis, how tennis was my life and how my self-worth was totally based on my tennis performance. When I would win a match or championship, the high would be great for a minute. But, all too soon, the emptiness would creep in again.

Conversely, I thought God certainly couldn't love a loser, and He'd already shown me that He was mad at me anyway. So when I would lose a match, my whole self-worth would plummet because, after all, my identity was completely wrapped up in tennis. And why was that so? Because it represented my mom, her memory, her legacy.

But Susan told me that I didn't have to perform for God. She said that God loved me no matter how well (or poorly!) I performed.

Instead she said, "God loves us so unconditionally that He sent His son, Jesus Christ, to die for our sins."

Furthermore, she said, by believing in Christ, I could be assured of an eternal destination in heaven. All I needed to do was to make a profession of faith by putting my trust in Him.

Susan asked me if I'd ever done that. I said no, I hadn't.

That God actually loved me that much was a staggering thought. Those words freed me. A great weight lifted off my heart and shoulders to know that I didn't have to earn God's love, that I didn't have to win tennis matches, for Him to love me.

After four hours of talking, I got on my knees and accepted Jesus Christ as my Lord and Savior. When I went home, I stayed up all night studying the scriptures Susan had given me. I didn't even look at the textbook. I didn't even think about the exam.

The next day, bleary-eyed, I went and took the exam. The answers I wrote differed in some areas to what I had been taught in class. I knew that I'd probably get a reaction from Dr. Thornton.

Three days later, Dr. Thornton called me into his office.

"Cindy, you are one of my top students. Don't we have a good relationship?"

"Oh yes, Dr. Thornton, we have a very good relationship."

"Cindy, you know, I can kind of tell in my class how things are going based on your response. If you have questions, I know that maybe I'm not being clear. But Cindy, at any time in this class, did you raise your hand?"

"No sir, I did not."

"At any time during this class, did you challenge me on what I had to say?"

"No sir, I didn't."

"At any time in this class, did you ever indicate once, even once, that perhaps what I was teaching was contrary to some of your beliefs?"

"No sir. No sir, I didn't."

By this point, he was a little annoyed with me. "Then, Cindy, on this exam, why have you challenged—in part—what I've taught?"

I wasn't meaning to defy Dr. Thornton. There was no spirit of condemnation in my exam answers, just the new-found truth I had learned twelve hours before.

I said, "Dr. Thornton, let me tell you about what happened to me last night."

I am so grateful that God used Dr. Thornton's class to expose me to the life-changing message of Jesus Christ.

Almost immediately, my perspective began to change. When you find that new faith, something changes in you—your heart is transformed. All of a sudden I looked at things differently. I was always responsible, so it wasn't like I was changing a behavior. What was changing, though, was what people would see in me. Perhaps it was a new sense of security or confidence that resulted from knowing that God loved me no matter what my circumstances were or how crummy my performance was. I *needed* to know that.

Upon graduation from Greenhill in 1975, I chose the University of Virginia over tennis powerhouses in California, Florida, and Texas. Tennis had just gone from an intramural sport to a full-fledged scholarship sports program at U.Va. But it wasn't the tennis I was seeking so much—it was the college experience. U.Va. had only gone co-ed in 1970, and while I loved the boy/girl ratio, what really attracted me was that it allowed a young woman—if she had any kind of leadership capabilities at all—to really make things happen. I was offered the first female tennis scholarship at U.Va. After talking with my dad, we decided to give my scholarship back to the university so that it could be used to recruit some of the top junior players who had played nationally with me.

During the four years I had the pleasure to be on the tennis team, U.Va. went from a fledgling intercollegiate tennis program to being ranked twelfth in the nation. It was a thrill to be part of that success.

I loved my four years at U.Va.—the university that Thomas Jefferson built is a terrific educational institution. I grew by leaps and bounds in so many areas of my life. Even though I was the number one player on the tennis team for most of my four years, there was not the pressure of being Little Mo's daughter. Very little was actually written about it. In fact, while I was in my fourth year at U.Va., NBC released a made-for-TV movie about Mom, *Little Mo*. I had a small part in the movie, but there was no press about it on the university grounds. I appreciated the lack of hype.

As a result, I grew and flourished, living on my own for the first time just being Cindy. The awards I won while at U.Va., as well as the mistakes I made, were clearly mine. I enjoyed the responsibility, the freedom, the relation-ships—and the relative anonymity.

But for all of my activities at U.Va., I still missed Mom. My dad was a great mother as well as a great father to me. My roommates would call their mothers. I would call Dad, but this was a busy time in his professional life. Men are wonder-ful, but women nurture and relate. There is only so much you can share with the best of dads, even though my dad was a very sensitive communicator who intuitively tracked with Brenda and me. He just seemed to sense our needs.

For example, one summer day I was home from my first year at U.Va., and I had some romance meltdown. (As I write this, I can't remember who it was concerning, but I am sure it was terribly traumatic at the time!) I couldn't sleep so I decided to bake—at 1:00 in the morning. I was convinced that cakes, brownies, and cookies tasted better if baked after 1:00 AM. So there I was, in the kitchen, at 1:00 AM. The kitchen was a long way from Dad's bedroom, but I was mak-ing such a noise banging pots and pans that it probably woke up the next-door neighbors!

He called from his bedroom, "Honey, what are you doing in there?"

"Nothing, dad. Everything's all right."

"Honey, why don't you come back here and let's talk about it?"

I went to his room and plopped on this bed.

"Is something bothering you, sweetheart? Let's talk about it."

So we talked.

About two hours later, at 3:00 in the morning, Dad said, "Now honey, is there anything else you need to tell me? Are you sure there's nothing else? Have we gotten this all taken care of?"

"Oh, Dad, thank you so much, I feel so much better. You're so wonderful."

"Now honey, if you're really okay, then I think I'd better go to sleep because I have an important meeting in the morning."

Then I went off to bed and, of course, I slept in.

Dad got up at 6:00 AM, so he had a total of three hours sleep. I later learned that he was meeting key executives from the Pillsbury Company to discuss the sale of Steak & Ale to their company. It was one of the most important meetings of his entire career. But he was willing to meet me where I was despite his personal sacrifice. That's the kind of dad I have. He's the best.

Dad really listened to Brenda and me. At the same time, I can only imagine his own emotional challenges. He was bearing his own heartache, trying to encourage Brenda and me and running a very successful restaurant chain. My dad is a superhero, but even the very best have their vulnerabilities.

God created distinct and separate roles for men and women. Moms are the nurturers. I grieved a lot in college, because I missed that relationship. Even though Dad would call me at U.Va., it just didn't have the same emotional impact.

I didn't really talk about my boyfriends that much with Dad. Why? Well, number one, I didn't know if Dad would approve. Number two, dads see things differently:

"Um, Dad, I'm seeing this new guy. He's kind of neat."

"What does his father do? What are his plans for the future? What's he majoring in?"

"Philosophy."

"Philosophy!"

Dad would sputter around about someone trying to make a living from philosophy. That sort of thing was not really important to a young girl enjoying college life with no more regard for the future than what time was her tennis match the next day or how many hours she had left before her next paper was due.

A mom, on the other hand, would ignore the new guy's major altogether and ask, "How does he treat you? Is he fun to be with? Does he like your double fudge brownies?"

That's the conversation I missed having, and *would* have had with Mom. Just girl-to-girl. Besides, I really would have loved to tell her how irresistible my double fudge brownies were!

When I graduated, I played the European professional tennis circuit for a summer. But it really wasn't for me. Most of my tennis friends turned pro, but I needed roots and relationships. Also, the difference between being a good college player and being a pro was a huge, huge chasm.

Somewhere in there, I realized that professional tennis wasn't my calling. Tennis had been a wonderful blessing in my life. It had filled a void, taught me discipline, given me a healthy self-esteem, and earned the respect of my peers. That success had provided tremendous opportunities for travel and meeting people who enriched my life. It had given me a purpose and had kept Mom's memory alive. I had grown to love the sport, but so much of that love was wrapped up in my desperate desire to hold on to my mother.

There are seasons in men's and women's lives that are really important. And Mom missed mine. No matter how good things were, I always kept thinking, "The sad thing is, Mom would have been here. Mom *should* have been here. *Mom, why aren't you here?*" And, there were so many times I would face a decision and wonder, "What would Mom say? What would Mom do? How would Mom react?" I would have "Mom" talks in my head, theorizing what she would say if she and I were talking about certain issues that needed resolution.

I left Europe, came back to Texas, and was ready to work. My first job was as a political consultant. I worked for a fine company, but it began to get a little uncomfortable because the people the firm represented were on one side of the political spectrum and I was on the other.

In May 1980, I began working at Willow Bend Polo and Hunt Club in Plano, Texas, at a time when that part of Collin County was rapidly growing. Willow Bend was a country club with active equestrian, tennis, fitness, and polo programs. Those were the golden years of Willow Bend, and I met a lot of people who are still important in my life today.

In the fall of 1980, I founded what at that time was called "A Weekend at Willow Bend to Wipe Out Cancer," a nonprofit organization to benefit the Collin County American Cancer Society. To raise money, we had a bake sale, T-shirt sales, a tennis and swim marathon, a horse show, and even a dance marathon. I got Willow Bend's membership involved and utilized the club's expansive facilities. My goal was to raise $2,000 the first year; we raised $6,000.

The next year the club members said, "Cindy, we need to do this again."

At that moment, I realized that "A Weekend at Willow Bend to Wipe Out Cancer" was the fulfillment of the resolve I'd made at my mom's funeral service—to crusade against cancer.

Today, a little more than twenty years later, from those humble beginnings we now have a full-time director of special events and hundreds of volunteers. We've raised approximately $2 million. The organization is now called Wipe Out Kids' Cancer and we benefit specific pediatric cancer research projects at Children's Medical Center of Dallas. It's one of the largest pediatric cancer nonprofits in North Texas. I've given the balance of my non-working life to this charity. But I consider all the sacrifice a joy because it is in memory of Mom, and I am touched beyond measure that so many people and sponsors have participated in our mission to eradicate childhood cancer.

Actually, Wipe Out Kids' Cancer is more than just a fundraiser, it's a ministry of sorts. Our volunteers encourage and pray with the cancer patients and their families at the hospital, if they are receptive to that. Each year, Children's Medical Center selects approximately ten ambassadors for Wipe Out Kids' Cancer. These ambassadors are children currently undergoing cancer treatments and range in age from six to sixteen. Wipe Out Kids' Cancer has a full schedule of events throughout the year for our ambassadors, including an annual summer swim party to which all alumni ambassadors and their families are invited. Over the years, many parents of our ambassadors have said that our program helped keep their children alive because it gave them hope and a future. I am deeply grateful for that!

But even with a rewarding, challenging job and numerous extracurricular activities to keep me occupied and—apparently—fulfilled, I knew something was missing. A restlessness followed me from college to Europe and back to Texas. I felt strong intellectually, physically, emotionally. I had lots of friends. But the spiritual component was missing. I began my search again to try to make sense of what had happened in my life—a life spent now as much without my mother as with her. Even though I had made my profession of faith at age sixteen, I really hadn't been nurtured in that faith. I desperately needed to be fed.

My search led me to Spring Valley United Methodist Church, which is where my grandmother attended until she died in 1980. Soon I got involved teaching a sixth grade confirmation class because I wanted to learn more about the basics of faith. I started to read the Word daily. From there, I began going to a weekly Bible study. The Bible study was led by a godly man and ordained minister, Don Anderson. Don and I developed a wonderful friendship.

I began to understand that even when Mom breathed her last breath, God was there. I began to understand that during college, God was using me. A number of my fellow students at U.Va. went through the same loss I did during college—a parent died and they didn't know how to deal with that death. I was able to counsel them and encourage them.

In the Bible study and in my new prayer life, I began to see that God really did have a purpose and a plan for my life through all of this. I still missed my mom terribly, and I still had big question marks. However, my mindset was beginning to change.

It was time to let Mom rest in peace.

At age twenty-five, thirteen years after Mom's passing, I went back to Mom's gravesite with Don Anderson and his wife, Pearl. We went through the burial service all over again.

Don said, "You can ruin the rest of your life by not being willing to let go of the past. Life's greatest challenge is what you are going to do with what's left."

Don was right. I had simply been postponing my grief over the past thirteen years. I hadn't wanted to say goodbye. I hadn't wanted to move on. I had only wanted Mom alive again.

So I had kept her alive by never mentally burying her. I was ruining a special part of my life by not letting go. Hanging on to the past was impacting my present positive relationships, including—and most importantly—my relationship with God.

During this second funeral service, Don made me say, "My mom is dead."

It took me two hours. I didn't want to admit that Mom was gone—and that I'd never see her again on this side of heaven.

After two hours of prayers and tears, I was able to utter those devastating words, "My mom is dead."

Painfully, I repeated those words. A soothing calmness overcame me and the hurt and anguish seemed to ease. Finally, I had the closure I so desperately needed.

And never knew I wanted until then.

Life after Loss

"Eagerness makes you work hard and hard work overcomes a lot of things which don't come naturally."
—Maureen Connolly Brinker

I had come to an important crossroads in my life. I had come to a degree of closure on my mother's death. What a difference that made! It was as if a part of me was freed from bondage. My emotions were released from dwelling on the past and I was now able to move forward, cherishing the wonderful memories of my mother rather than being saddened by them.

The air was clearer, the days were brighter and my broken heart was on the mend. It was time to move on with my emotions intact.

Over the next couple of years, I relished my work at Willow Bend Polo and Hunt Club as director of membership and special events. I genuinely enjoyed greeting each person who came by to request membership information. It was exciting being part of Willow Bend's explosive growth. And I found a niche developing and publicizing events at the club. From creating the diverse member activities and half-time extravaganzas at the Sunday polo matches, to promoting club memberships to the rapidly expanding community of Plano that now surrounded the confines of Willow Bend, I began to see this as my professional calling, something that meshed with my talents and my personality. Besides, it was fun!

At the same time, I was digesting what had just happened in my life. After five rewarding years, I left Willow Bend and took some time to write as much as I could remember about my mom's life. My goal was to save as many of those precious memories and insights as possible.

During that time, I received a number of outside requests to publicize events and handle various public relations projects—I suppose because of the success I'd had at doing just that at Willow Bend.

At first, I forwarded these calls to Sissy Jeffett, who was a whiz at event management and media relations. Sissy was the daughter of Nancy Jeffett and was like a sister to me.

So when I finished chronicling my thoughts and memories, Sissy and I decided to start a public relations firm together in 1986—Brinker Jeffett & Associates. Our first event was the Virginia Slims of Dallas, which benefited the Maureen Connolly Brinker Tennis Foundation. We worked out of the tennis foundation's office and helped negotiate player contracts and organize various components of this Dallas-based professional women's tennis tournament.

Slowly, we secured other clients and our business grew.

Sissy married in 1989 and moved to Memphis. I bought out her interest and waited a year to change the name of the firm to Brinker Communications out of deference to Sissy.

When I first started in business, Dad wanted to know, "Cindy, are you self-employed or unemployed?" The second year he wanted to know, "Honey, just remind me: are you for profit or not-for-profit?" Now he's quit asking, although in the early years it felt more like a not-for-profit organization than I would have liked! At times during those years our employees made more than I did!

But fifteen years later, business is robust for our full-service public relations company and I am blessed to have a talented team of communications specialists working with me.

Brinker Communications specializes in media relations, strategic marketing and branding, corporate communications, special events/promotions, and advertising. We also work a great deal with nonprofit organizations, typically through companies that want to benefit them while hiring us to launch their new products or promote their services. Nonprofits also hire us directly.

Our firm is also asked to publicize numerous events of all sizes. Most of them—not surprisingly—benefit a charity. We really enjoy that aspect of our work because civic involvement is in keeping with Brinker Communications' corporate culture.

One thing that has been a constant over the years is my involvement with Wipe Out Kids' Cancer. Our mission still remains to benefit specific pediatric cancer research projects at Children's Medical Center of Dallas. Children's is internationally recognized for its innovative work in childhood cancer research and treatment. In fact, initial funding for some of Children's most internationally noted cancer research projects came from Wipe Out Kids' Cancer. What a privilege it is to pursue a cure and make a difference in the lives of these remarkable children with cancer.

Because philanthropy is such a passion of mine (I learned from the best role models possible—my mother and my father), I've had the honor of serving on many local nonprofit boards. I consider it a pleasure to serve my community.

Again, that goes back to the lessons Mom and Dad taught me about how vitally important it is to invest in the lives of others. Giving back is one of my fundamental beliefs. It is something that was planted, nurtured, and exemplified by both of my parents. They didn't just talk about helping others, they *acted*.

In the midst of all of this activity, I was focused exclusively on my career. Oh, I dated, but my real energy went into building Brinker Communications.

When I was still working at Willow Bend, I asked Don Anderson, the minister I had the "re-funeral" with, to teach a Bible study at the country club in 1983. At first, we had ten people in attendance, but the general manager Buzz Welker was very supportive and within a year we had a hundred-plus people. By this time, the Bible study was being hosted at Buzz's home on Willow Bend's property. People were on top of people, but it was a lot of fun worshipping together every Wednesday evening.

One night, a very handsome man walked into the Bible study, and to this day Bob Simmons does not know how he got there. But there he was. I believe it was an angel who told him to come.

I was just taken by Bob. He had been on the staff of Campus Crusade for Christ for four years and now he was helping establish an organization to assist companies in North Texas to export goods worldwide. We soon became great friends. We were best friends for seven years, and I continually compared the other boyfriends I had to Bob. But it never dawned on me to do something to ruin our great relationship—like date him! Bob was like a big brother to me. His sister Katina also became my best friend. At the time, she was working for Campus Crusade for Christ and its Athletes in Action program in California.

It wasn't long before I became an unofficial member of the Simmons family. In fact, his adorable mother Pauline began to say she had three children when asked about her family. Because Dad and Mom were only children, Brenda and I had no aunts, uncles, or cousins. On the other hand, Pauline was one of ten children. As a result, I enjoyed going with Katina and Bob to their family reunions. I was so excited about going to my first family reunion with them that I memorized all of the names of Bob's aunts, uncles, cousins, and second cousins!

Year after year I went, but always as a friend, not as a girl-friend. However, everybody else on both sides of the family seemed to know we'd get together long before we knew it.

Bob and I married in 1990 after seven years of best friendship. The great thing is, we're still best friends today. And just as when I first met Bob at the Bible study, God drew us together and has been at the center of our relationship ever since. Our marriage is based on our love for our Savior first and each other second. This priority fuels our romance.

In short, life was great. My marriage was everything I'd dreamed it would be. My job was rewarding and fulfilling. Bob and I were immersed in charity and church work.

In a single, heartbreaking moment, that all changed.

Polo is the second most dangerous sport in the world, next to car racing. Dad always said, "It's not a matter of 'if' a person playing polo will have an accident, it's a matter of when."

It's the same in life: it's not a matter of *if* you're going to get hurt deeply, emotionally—it's a matter of *when*. Crises happen just as life happens. It could be the death of a parent, a child, a spouse, a close friend. It could be a divorce. It could be the loss of a business and bankruptcy. It could be a dramatic health reversal. It could be a crippling accident. But some day, perhaps some day soon, something unexpected will occur that tests you to the core of your being.

In 1993, almost twenty-four years after Mom's passing, I thought that I'd already been through the toughest patch of my life.

That's when I received the telephone call. The date was January 21, 1993. It was late on a Thursday evening.

Earlier that afternoon, my dad had had a serious polo accident in Palm Beach, Florida. I later saw a videotape of the accident. Dad's horse Omega got "T-boned" by another horse. A third horse was charging up on the line of the polo ball and as that horse continued up the field, Dad was blindsided by another horse charging straight at him, whose path had been blocked by the horse on the line of the ball. There was a horrific collision.

At that moment, Dad's horse had three legs off the ground in a full run. Dad had no chance. He was hurtled off his horse and slammed into the ground. Fortunately, he was wearing a state-of-the-art polo helmet. Still, the impact from the collision rammed his head into the polo field and Omega fell on top of him. Omega panicked and began thrashing wildly about, trying to get up. Repeatedly, the horse's instability sent him crashing back on top of Dad.

We were fortunate that Dad was not paralyzed, but he was comatose with a head injury. Perhaps the hardest thing about head injuries is the uncertainty. Dad could be in a coma for three days, three weeks, three years, or forever. It's not like cancer where, if you receive a certain treatment, the patient may experience a more predictable outcome. With a coma, *nothing* is predictable.

Hour after hour, there was no change. Dad was still alive—but just barely. Breathing tubes were keeping him alive. He was not appearing to make any progress. Two of the five doctors said there was no chance of recovery from the coma. They said he would probably be dead in four to six days. Two others held out a little hope—Dad would regain only a small part of his faculties—tops. The fifth said that since Dad was so physically fit, he would probably be paralyzed on the left side and would be in the hospital from one to two years—but that he would eventually regain his total faculties.

Dad's situation continued to deteriorate. At one point on Friday evening, the doctors didn't think he was going to live through the night.

So early Saturday morning, I flew to Palm Beach. It was the longest trip of my life.

Arriving at the hospital, I prepared myself to go see Dad. It was painful. He was hooked up to a number of monitors in ICU, his chest heaving up and down in a loud and consistent breathing cycle. His features were distorted and it looked like he'd been badly beaten.

A month before the accident, Dad took a stress test to determine his fitness level. His tests showed that he had the body of a forty-year-old. At the time of the accident, he was sixty-one. When I saw him, he looked like a different person. This battered and nearly lifeless man couldn't be my father.

That night, feeling so scared and helpless, I got down on my hands and knees and cried out to God. I bargained with God. I said, "God, take me. Take me in Dad's place."

All of a sudden, God spoke to me. My Lord and Savior spoke to me.

He said, "Cindy, my dear child, why are you doing this? You don't need to bargain with Me. I'm God. Your father will come out of his coma. He will live."

I was awe-struck. Nothing like this had ever happened to me before. I was frozen in fear, yet bathed in comfort. I knelt there trembling, still listening, scarcely daring to breathe.

Then the Word was gone.

But it was so real; it was as real as the bowl of Raisin Bran I'd eaten that morning for breakfast, as real as anything I'd ever experienced in my life.

And I stood on that. An extraordinary peace washed over me.

The next day, our family met with the doctors again. They said, "I'm sorry, but Mr. Brinker has about a 10 to 20 percent chance of coming out of this coma."

In a very gentle way, I disagreed with them.

I said, "Let's not look at the 80 to 90 percent chance he has of dying or not coming out of the coma. Let's look at the 10 to 20 percent chance he has of living."

I was so filled with God's peace from the night before that I *knew* Dad was going to live. The doctors were talking Greek to me, their predictions seemed so unrealistic.

Even when I came back to Dallas a week later, I told my office staff, "Dad's going to live. This is not a death sentence. Dad's going to come out of this."

When I was not sitting by Dad in ICU or visiting with my family on that first visit, I wandered the halls of the hospital. It was at this time that I met a couple. The wife's brother had fallen down a flight of stairs, striking his head. He, too, was comatose. I befriended this couple and we prayed each time we were together. But soon it became clear that her brother would never emerge from his coma. In time, they faced the awful prospect of pulling all life support from this dear brother. His injury, on the surface at least, appeared so much less severe than Dad's injury.

In the end, they instructed their doctors to cut off all life support systems. As traumatic as it was, I was thankful God placed me there to pray with them during their hours of greatest need.

Three weeks later, because of the damage caused by Dad's throat tube, the doctors scheduled a tracheotomy for 3:00 PM that day.

He woke up from his coma at 1:00 PM.

Now *that's* a God thing.

Not that you can't reverse a tracheotomy, but you just don't want a tracheotomy if there are other options.

I have no doubt that God spared Dad's life. God used talented people—good doctors, good nurses, good technicians. And my stepmother Nancy was very prudent in her decisions immediately after Dad's accident and during the recovery that followed. Likewise, Dad's great physical fitness helped save his life. But the reality is, God spared Dad's life. Period. To God goes all the glory and credit.

Dad's mind was scrambled when he first woke up. His sentences didn't quite make sense, but he was awake.

This was mid-February. As soon as he was able to focus clearly, Dad's main goal was to be back for a board meeting at his company on May 4. As usual, Mr. Problem Solver took over. When the doctors moved him to the Del Ray Rehabilitation Center in Florida, he had less than three months to be fully functional in time for that board meeting.

The physical therapists smiled and said, "Mr. Brinker, this could take a long time." Dad smiled back and kicked up his rehab to seven days a week of full-time physical therapy—with *no* interruptions.

By the end of April, Dad's recovery was more than remarkable, it was miraculous! It was the quickest progress of any patient the center had ever had. Before his accident, Dad had been selected to receive a prestigious award that was to be presented a few weeks prior to his May board meeting. At this point in his rehab, Dad would have been able to go and receive it, but he decided not to go. Instead, he wanted to rehab literally up to the day he left the center. Like everything Dad's involved with, when he sets a goal, it gets the full focus of his attention.

During the coma and during his rehabilitation, Dad received five thousand letters and cards. I received another five hundred, some to me, some to pass on to my dad. He'd read them, then work harder in his physical therapy.

Additionally, Dad's competitors frequently called to say, "Norman, you've got to get better. We need to have you back." Dad has fostered such love and respect from those within the restaurant business.

People really pulled for him.

And it worked.

Dad went to the May 4 board meeting of Brinker International and was officially reinstated as its chairman and chief executive officer. He did so with little fanfare. He had not wanted a big fuss. However, when Dad walked unassisted up to the doors of Brinker International's headquarters with only a slight limp in his left leg that betrayed his ordeal, a huge sign hung outside the building. It read, "Welcome back, Norman. We love you."

Dad still has physical therapy sessions. However, through it all, his spirits have never wavered. I was worried that he'd become bitter or depressed or frustrated that he was no longer able to do what he used to do athletically. After all, Dad was an Olympian. But Dad chose, as always, to be positive despite his circumstances. He told four hundred employees the day he came back to work that a key factor in his remarkable recovery was not feeling sorry for himself.

"Negative thinking is the first step backward and that means no progress," he said. "I was more excited about the good things that were happening. I wasn't depressed about the negative side of things."

In a way, that's how it was with my mom. Mom never wanted to accept the fact that she could be defeated by cancer. Her positive attitude kept her going because she was a champion. Champions move forward—compelled by their passion and perseverance to master the task at hand.

Dad never accepted anything less than he was going to have a full recovery. And through it all—like Mom—he carried on with grace and determination.

Slowly, life returned to normal in Dallas. Bob and I built a wonderful life together, my company continued to grow and Dad's health continually improved. I was nearly thirty-seven. I'd been married four years—with no kids. Every now and then, an insightful friend would ask, "Cindy, are you contemplating a family?"

"Bob and I are thinking about it."

"Well, what's keeping you from it?"

"Well, you know, we're busy."

And then that friend would pause and ask:

"Cindy, are you afraid of having a child and then dying?"

At first, I always said no.

But in time I realized that that was *exactly* what was happening. I was afraid. I did not want my child to experience what I'd been through. I didn't want my baby to be a motherless child.

Meanwhile, Bob and I were having a lot of fun together. We were working, traveling, involved in charities, and heavily committed to our church. Having children just seemed to be the last thing on our minds.

So rather than face my fear, I'd almost reconciled myself to the fact that I'd be a wonderful aunt. Brenda already had two children whom I adored.

My participation with Wipe Out Kids' Cancer continued to pick up speed. As mentioned earlier, each year, Children's Medical Center would select ten children with cancer to serve as our ambassadors and represent the hospital in all our nonprofit activities. Naturally, I was very involved in the lives of these precious and inspirational children. But sometimes—too often—cancer claimed the lives of some of our ambassadors. I have cried with the mothers, and I've gone to far too many funerals. Over the years, on my credenza, I have had pictures of children we've lost, children I'd spent loads of time with and really gotten to know. And now they were gone. My little heroes had gone on to glory and I missed them terribly. I think in the back of my mind, I was afraid to lose another child.

However, in 1995, with lots of loving encouragement from Bob, we did have a wonderful little boy, William Brinker Simmons.

But the minute our healthy, alert William was born, I had an even stronger resolve to work in the fight against childhood cancer.

In 1980, less than 50 percent of children with cancer survived. Today, just over 20 years later, children's cancer survival rates have increased to 75 percent and, in many cancers, have exceeded 90 percent. Cancer is the second leading cause of death among children aged one to fourteen years in the United States. (Accidents are first.)

But there is so much left to do. Wipe Out Kids' Cancer is dedicated to its mission of eradicating pediatric cancer— until survival rates are 100 percent. Cancer is not necessarily a death sentence. Most of our ambassadors live with the disease and go on to experience productive, happy, and fulfilling lives. However, I never get over losing our kids. I wouldn't want to.

William's arrival blessed Bob and me beyond measure. However, the first time I looked at our sweet son in his little bassinet, a new wave of sadness unexpectedly swept over me. I think it was then that it really hit me: My mom was not there to share this incredible day with me. By all rights, she should have been there. I just know that Mom would have been the most extraordinary grandmother. William would have adored her. They would have gotten along so well.

I'm sad that she missed my pregnancy and the arrival of our greatest joy. I had many close, dear friends to talk to, but I imagine there's nothing quite like being able to share your deepest fears and dreams with your mother. After all, babies don't come with instructions, and I was very green. And my mother wasn't there. How I missed her coaching me during this precious—and challenging—time of new motherhood. I know she would have been overjoyed with being a grandmother and mentoring me along the way. I could have learned so much from her in the days, weeks, months, and years following William's arrival—and William would have been the beneficiary of that counsel.

At every step of her life, Mom always wanted to learn. She deeply regretted that she never attended college. She went from high school to playing the most prestigious tournaments in the world. And when her career ended, she and my dad set a wedding date to coincide with her first major assignment covering Wimbledon for *The London Daily Mail*. (They had such fun honeymooning for two weeks, all expenses paid!) After their honeymoon, they settled in San Diego. It wasn't long before they had two beautiful children (at least that's what they always told us!). In short order, my dad jumped into the restaurant business, working for Jack-In-The-Box. From there, we moved to Phoenix, then to Houston as Dad was responsible for taking the Jack-In-The-Box concept eastward. It just never seemed to be the right time for Mom to go to college.

However, after many rewarding years with Jack-In-The-Box, Dad decided that we should move to Dallas to start his first restaurant, Brink's Coffee Shop (before he created Steak & Ale). We moved and it looked like we'd be in Dallas a while. (Actually, we have never left!) We didn't live far from

Southern Methodist University and, as soon as we got settled, Mom enrolled in college. She was a great believer in education and learning.

Dad said that Mom loved history, so that's what she studied. He recalled:

> Maureen was not able to get a college degree because of her tennis career. So when she finally went, she was a student *par excellence*. She managed to complete about two years worth of courses at SMU, going mainly at night, before her health deteriorated too far. She attacked college with the same concentration she displayed on the tennis courts. She knew exactly what she was taking and what she wanted to accomplish each day.

I recently found a charming letter from Mom to Dad's mother, Kathryn, dated February 19, 1964. Amid the family news of buying a new house in Dallas and my dad's work, she took a moment to type this letter on the eve of a big exam:

> I have been so negligent in writing you as of late. It is not because I do not think of you often but rather that the days are really full with a multitude of projects and the evenings are spent studying after the children are put down. Tomorrow evening we have our first test in Am. Hist. and I must make this relatively short so as to study adequately. Actually I feel prepared but there are a lot of last minute dates that I would like to finalize in my mind. Also have started working on the book report. Have decided to summarize 10 articles from *Am. Heritage* (which we may do as I think that it will be more interesting and something that most of the others will not do.) I just can't tell you what going to school means to me. Has given me a new direction in my life and is just the most rewarding thing that could have happened. One realizes how stagnant we can become over the years when we are not asked to use our memories and various faculties. At any rate, I am thrilled and so look forward to our two nights weekly.

Mom apprenticed herself all of her life. She looked for new opportunities and ways to stretch herself. She found great teachers, listened to them—and put into practice what she heard.

In her tennis career, Mom had two major coaches, Wilbur Folsom, who was her first coach, and Eleanor "Teach" Tennant.

I respect Wilbur so much because he saw Mom's potential when everyone else saw a quiet little girl with intense eyes clinging to the fence in San Diego's public courts. He took her as far as he could take her.

And then, what is most impressive about Wilbur, is when it became obvious that Mom was going to be a champion, he didn't say, "I can't take her any further, but I'm not going to let anybody else take her." Instead, he recommended that she meet with Eleanor "Teach" Tennant, who helped make her into a champion.

In her personal life, Mom was coached by my dad. When they got married, her tennis career was over. But a new, equally exciting dimension of her life was just beginning. "Little Mo" had turned into "Little Mom" and she and Dad were embarking on a new journey together—parenthood. In the fourteen years they were married, Dad coached Mom on communication skills and polishing her personal presentation.

In that respect, I've had many great coaches as well. We're all the sum of our parts. In life, every relationship, every challenge offers opportunities for learning. I've been very blessed in all my pivotal relationships: my dad, my sister, my tennis coaches, my husband, my little boy, my friends. But the most significant coach throughout my life—without even realizing it—has been my mom.

In sports terms, coaches get us in shape, help make us mentally tough, anticipate movements and shots, and encourage us to get the proper rest and nutrition we need. Good coaches do more than just instruct us on the fundamentals of a given sport, they teach us the importance of sportsmanship. They educate us about practicing the correct way and maximizing our gifts and talents. They help us with manners and etiquette, they help us understand relationships—and they help us understand the power of those relationships.

My coach, who was a world champion, taught me these lessons. I've tried to apply them on and off the court. Mom taught me lessons that applied not only to the playing field but to life as well. I am so grateful to have been on the receiving end of that love and counsel.

More than 30 years after Mom's death, she's just as real now as she was when I'd snuggle up next to her on the couch, drinking in the unconditional nature of her love, breathing her barest hint of perfume, and glorying in that sunny smile that was directed straight at me.

I remember my mom.

The lessons she taught me in her all-too-brief life are more precious than the most valuable treasures and are cherished beyond measure.

That is her legacy to me.

And because of who she was, I'm compelled to share those lessons.

Lessons from a remarkable woman who also happened to be a world champion.

My mom.

Maureen and Cindy, 1965

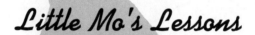

Little Mo's Lessons

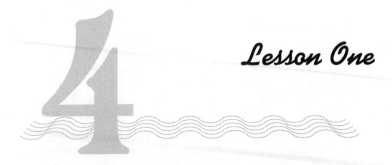

Lesson One

You Can't Always Control Your Circumstances, But You Can Control Your Responses to Those Circumstances

Many times, circumstances have been beyond my control, but my responses to those circumstances *are* something I can control.

Mom was so gracious and positive, even in dying, that her example would not allow me to be bitter.

Why? Because Mom dealt with dying the same way she dealt with living: by embracing it, by being strong, by being positive, by facing her fear with courage, by strategizing her road to victory and, most importantly, doing all of this in a humble manner. She would have been so disappointed if she thought that through her death I was grieving to the point of being immobilized or angry beyond reason.

That just wasn't her way. In *Forehand Drive*, Mom recalled with chilling detachment the accident on July 20, 1954, that ended her remarkable tennis career. She'd been riding Colonel Merry Boy with a friend, when suddenly a cement truck thundered over a rise and sideswiped her, sending horse and rider careening off the road. Mom lay stunned for a moment:

> As I started to rise, my right leg buckled. I managed to hop on my left leg to the side of the road, where I sat

> down. It was then that I noticed that blood had seeped through the leg of my riding togs, but I did not associate the sharp stinging sensation when the truck passed with the blood on my leg. Then I rolled up my trouser leg and saw my leg slashed to the bone, the flesh lying open. I screamed, started to cry, then I looked up. Colonel Merry Boy had returned and stood beside me looking down. He wasn't even scratched.
>
> "My tennis . . . my tennis . . . I'll never be able to play again," I thought hysterically. Then, calmly, there came the clear knowledge that this meant the end of my tennis career.

No railing against fate, no cursing the unfairness of it, just a clear-eyed realization that this was probably the end.

Dad's mother kept all of the newspaper accounts of Mom's accident and the days that followed, even though Dad and Mom were only engaged at the time. The headlines and articles were remarkably revealing about the kind of person she was.

For instance, *The Chicago Daily News'* headline from July 21, 1954 read "'Little Mo' Hurt, but Keeps Smiling:"

> Maureen Connolly, 19-year-old women's tennis champion, was reported 'cheerful and smiling' despite a broken leg which will keep her from defending her National title at Forest Hills next month.

This article from *The Arizona Daily Star* is in a similar vein:

> Hospitalized Little Mo Jokes with Newsmen, Tennis Champ In Good Spirits, Doing Well After Suffering Broken Leg in Accident.

The unnamed reporter's article claimed that Mom was alert and kidded with the assembled newsmen and photographers:

> I am in great shape except for my leg. This is the first time I have been photographed lying on my back.

At the time, Mom wrote a weekly article for her hometown newspaper, *The San Diego Union,* called "Letter from Li'l Mo."

Just two weeks after the accident, she filed this report in a column with the headline, "Week in Hospital a New Experience":

> You know a week in a hospital can be kinda fun and I really enjoyed kibitzing with the student nurse and taking my fill of a favorite pastime – loafing. Now, at the age of 19, 'old rockin' chair's got me,' but not for long folks, not for long . . .

> . . . There is an old saying that when you're in trouble friends will make themselves known, and how true it is! Your many telegrams [Mom received over five hundred during her stay in the hospital], flowers, letters, and gifts that arrived daily gave me much encouragement and the realization of so many friends. Maureen Connolly really is the luckiest girl on earth.

Oh, she fought the rockin' chair, of course.

But what amazes me is that until this point, when she realized her career was over, Mom's entire identity appeared to be wrapped up in her status as a tennis player. (In 1952, she even wrote "tennis player" in the section of her passport that asked for "occupation.")

And now, in the seconds that transpired after her one-sided confrontation with the cement truck, her identity had vanished. Life—as she had always known it, as the world had always known it—was forever altered. Yet, in the pain and stark realization of that horrifying truth, *she chose joy!*

Mom was not just some weekend tennis hacker, she was the world champion—twice over.

And now, everything was different.

Not even twenty, her maturity and tremendous inner strength of character produced a positive response rather than bitterness, humor rather than self-pity. In spite of her dire circumstances, Mom chose joy.

I doubt my response would have been without some sort of complaining or feeling sorry for myself. Not Mom. Not even a whimper.

Not that she gave up without a gallant fight. For months after the accident, she rehabbed religiously. She did everything possible for a comeback that spring, including taking ballet lessons to strengthen her leg. She wrote of picking up "millions" of marbles with her toes, trying to rebuild the muscles.

However, when she was finally able to return to the courts, she was not satisfied with the way her injured right leg responded in tennis practice. She was concerned about what would happen to the leg under the strain of no-holds-barred tournament play. Even one-legged, Mom could have still played at a very high level. But Mom was the world champion. And simply playing at "a very high level" was just not good enough.

Mom's tennis career officially came to an end when she announced her retirement from tournament play on February 22, 1955. And, as before, she dwelt on the positive. She told the press, "I think I would enjoy trying to pass on the things I have learned to other hopefuls. And who knows, perhaps I may be able to help another young girl along to championships such as I have enjoyed myself?"

"The leg was never good enough for tournament play again," Ben Press once told me, "although it held up pretty well for exhibitions. The first time we played after her accident, she had to stop and rub the circulation back into that leg—it had turned blue while we were volleying. But I never once heard her curse her luck. She repeatedly told me, 'I have no regrets.'

"Maureen could have set records that would never be broken because she had such a running start at that age on everyone who would ever follow her. The way things are now, that streak will probably never happen like that again.

"It didn't matter to Maureen. Even though it was clear that she wasn't happy with the situation, she never once said, 'Why me?' All her life, she had a super attitude."

Mom exhibited an attitude of gratitude for what tennis had done for her, the places she had been, and the people she had met. There was no room for self-pity. Instead, she chose joy. She accepted the present and looked forward to the future instead of looking back at the past. She was at peace with her circumstances and chose to greet each new day with a smile.

Mom's response was so positive, how could I dare respond differently? Would she want me to wrap myself in bitterness or resignation? No way! After all, she had demonstrated how she had responded when bad things happened. Her courage still awes me.

In this drama called life, Mom isn't the only person who has taught this lesson. In 1985, I was among the tens of thousands who read of a father and mother whose tragedy was to reach nightmarish proportions. Yet, how they responded still continues to inspire me, many years later.

Their names are Laurie and Ed Bolden. Ed and Laurie had a son, Allen. If you lived in the Dallas-Fort Worth area in June of 1985, you probably read about Allen. At seventeen, he was a nationally ranked swimmer with a scholarship to begin studies at Texas Christian University that fall. Some say Allen was an Olympic hopeful. He was smart, popular, handsome, and dearly loved by his family.

But late one Friday night in June, Allen didn't return home from a summer job as a lifeguard at a local public pool.

His parents were frantic. The local media followed every move of the police department's frenzied search.

Three days later, Allen's battered body was found. Two eighteen-year-old boys were later charged with kidnapping, robbing, and killing Allen.

As horrific as that crime was, I'll never forget the courage of Laurie and Ed Bolden. They faced a sea of news reporters with extraordinary composure.

"It's like losing a leg," Laurie said. "I have this gigantic wound that has to heal or I'll die. I have learned that nothing is mine, nothing at all but my faith in God. Everything else is a gift."

In the face of a loss that seemed too immense to comprehend, Laurie and Ed held fiercely to their faith.

And then Ed said something that continues to resonate and hearten me to this day. He said, "Pain is mandatory. Suffering is optional."

The Boldens had no control over this tragic circumstance, but they did have control over their response to that circumstance.

Their response: Pain is mandatory, suffering is optional.

What they were saying was that pain happens in life. How we allow that pain to infiltrate and eventually dominate our lives or *not* dominate our lives will dictate the quality of life we lead and the degree of suffering we experience. Our responses to our circumstances influence whether we are victorious or defeated in life. It's a matter of choice.

Life is a drama played out with its joys and sorrows, victories and defeats. Life is about wildly varying circumstances and our responses to those circumstances. It's about responding the same way in sickness and in health, in poverty and in wealth, and in good times as well as in bad times.

So what should our response be?

It *should* be Mom's example to me—I can't control the circumstances, but I can choose joy despite the heartache that comes my way.

It *should* be Ed Bolden's courageous declaration in the face of a heart-stopping loss: pain is mandatory—suffering is optional.

Brenda vividly remembered that Mom was always positive despite her sickness. Mom was still giving speeches up to two or three months before she died. Mom did not let her circumstances change her. She did not allow her circumstances to detour her.

"We still had kids in the house, she was still doing so much with herself, focusing on others rather than wallowing in her own pain and pity," Brenda recalls. "I just never knew she was so sick."

Nancy Jeffett tells a story about an incident that occurred a few months before Mom's death:

"The Maureen Connolly Brinker Mixed Doubles charity tournament was a big social occasion in Dallas and Maureen desperately wanted it to be a continued success," Nancy said. "She was already terribly ill and had had a blood transfusion that morning but didn't tell anybody. She was determined to take part in all of the festivities and socializing of the tournament.

"Eventually, though, she became terribly weak and collapsed. I took her inside the clubhouse of the Dallas Country Club where the tournament was taking place and helped her on to a cot in the back. She was in terrible pain. But once she'd mastered it, she insisted on getting up and going back out. She even made a little talk. Her will was really incredible. She didn't want anybody to know she had collapsed."

Mom didn't want to disappoint the people who had taken the time to participate in her namesake tournament. She didn't want to allow her pain to spoil the magic of the moment. She thought about everyone else first and relegated her misery to a non-issue.

Nancy said that she took Mom back to the hospital a few days later.

"She was so desperately sick and in such severe pain all of the way to the hospital," Nancy recalled. "She crawled in the back seat and laid down, so ill she was doubled over in terrible pain. And all of the while, whenever she could catch her breath, she apologized for the inconvenience!

"Despite the unbelievable pain, she was always thinking about somebody else."

In her final days, Mom tried to reach as many of her friends as possible. One of the first people she called was Ben Press.

"The last time I talked with her was two days before she died," Ben recalled. "Maureen knew she was dying. She called me from the hospital, with only days left. And what's amazing is that she didn't have one bit of bitterness. Instead, she talked about what a great life she'd had, what a great husband she had, what wonderful children she had—and how fortunate she was. Maureen was totally grateful for the life she did have. Then she talked about all of the things we did together and what she accomplished.

"I'm still somewhat awed that our last conversation was totally upbeat, that there wasn't a trace of anger in her voice. She knew there was not a lot of time, and yet she repeatedly told me how grateful she was that she had her family.

"Not one time did I hear her ask, 'Why me?'"

Nancy Jeffett received a similar call. Again, the focus of the conversation continued to turn from Mom to what Nancy was doing.

"Even in the hours before her death, she was thinking of somebody else," Nancy said. "I never heard her complain. Maureen was really a remarkable person, an incredible woman."

There is a lady whom I have never met, but read about in *The Dallas Morning News* a number of years ago who, like Mom, epitomizes "grace under fire" to me. Her name is Linda Kearbey. Linda was thirty years old when she was driving one morning on a foggy Missouri highway. All of a sudden, a large truck came barreling down her side of the highway and smashed head on into her small car. The impact of the crash shoved the engine of Linda's car through the firewall. The bones in Linda's left leg were shattered. Her right leg was fractured both above and below the knee. She also suffered grave internal injuries.

Through her pain, Linda heard the state trooper who inspected the wreckage say, "She'll never make it."

Linda spent all but twenty days of the next year in a veteran's administration hospital. She endured four months on the critical list, two months in intensive care. Her pancreas didn't function for several weeks.

Linda fought through a very slow, tough recovery and had fifteen surgeries in all. At first, her doctors said she wouldn't live, then she wouldn't get out of bed, then she wouldn't walk. But they underestimated Linda's resiliency and spirit.

"I decided it was too hard to fight the depression and the disability," Linda later said. "So I forgot about handling the depression and dealt with the disability as I went along."

After a long and torturous rehabilitation, Linda surprised everyone except herself. She got out of bed, she stood, she walked.

But the story doesn't end there. Her legs stubbornly refused to mend. In the two years that followed, doctors were eventually forced first to amputate the left leg at the thigh, then removed the other leg below the knee.

Linda recognized that she had a choice on how she would spend the rest of her life and she has chosen to live it to the fullest.

"I'm only as handicapped as I want to be,' she said. Then, she added with a twinkle in her eye, "I'm on my way to heaven."

The reporter asked a final question: "And how do you know about your ultimate destination with such certainty?"

Linda smiled: "I've already got two feet there."

For Linda, suffering was optional because she chose to respond that way. She chose joy in her life despite her circumstances. Just like Mom.

Pain is mandatory, suffering is optional.

It's a choice.

5

Lesson Two

Practice, Practice, Practice!

After Mom won her first U.S. Open Women's Championship in 1951, the organizers of the tournament held a ceremonial courtside presentation for the women's winner and runner-up. But shortly before the presentation on center court, Mom was nowhere to be found. The tournament organizers started to panic. They combed Forest Hills, the complex in New York where the U.S. Open was once played. (The championships are now held in Flushing Meadow.) She wasn't in the clubhouse, she wasn't in the locker room, she wasn't in the press room, she was nowhere in the central confines of Forest Hills.

Finally, on the most remote back court, a few people heard the slap of tennis balls popping. They followed the sound and there was Little Mo, with her coach, hitting overheads.

Mom had determined that her overheads had not been up to her exacting standards during the championship match, so immediately she and Teach Tennant had found a secluded court on which to practice. And in the process, she'd lost track of time.

Mom had just won the U.S. Open. She is the second youngest woman in the history of tennis to have ever done so. She was the number one women's tennis player in the United States. And there she was, systematically hitting overheads because she did not feel her overheads had been of championship caliber in her match!

Mom believed in practice.

Practice, it is said, makes perfect.

I believe it. There's no way to cut corners. If you're going be the best at what you're best at, you've got to practice. On the tennis court, the champion isn't the person who practices an hour a day or every other day. It's the person who methodically, steadily, sacrificially goes out and practices. It's the person who practices his/her weak shots, not just his/her strengths. It's the person who goes out and practices when it hurts.

When I was ten, I started taking tennis lessons. Mom and Dad never wanted to push me in that area, but it was just natural that I would someday be interested in playing tennis. After my first few lessons, the inevitable happened. I couldn't hit a ball over the net. I came in the kitchen after a particularly grueling lesson, and in a fit of frustration, I threw down my tennis racket. It clattered loudly across the linoleum floor.

Mom was reading a book at the kitchen table. When I threw down my racket, she looked up in a jolt, quite startled.

I walked up to her with my hands on my hips and with all of the diplomacy of a stampeding ten-year-old, I said, "Mommy, when you were number one in the world, did you stop taking tennis lessons?"

Still sitting, she drew me up to her until I was looking down at those twinkling brown eyes of hers. She said, "Honey, the day I would have stopped taking tennis lessons would have been the day I would have stopped being number one in the world."

That has stuck with me, both in my business career and in my personal life. What Mom was saying was that whenever you stop desiring to learn, to grow, to improve, when you start believing your own press, that's when you stop learning, growing, and improving.

There are no shortcuts. You must practice, practice, and practice some more. You have to keep learning.

For all of us, in any profession, whether it's on the playing field, in the board room, or as a homemaker, we need to constantly learn more about what we're doing. We can never stop improving our skills. To understand how to become a better parent we need to be continually reading, listening, asking questions, spending time with our children. Whatever our calling, we must be on a continuous learning curve, seeking every day how to be wiser and more skilled at what we are doing.

And that's the way it was with Mom. She never stopped improving, even when she was the world champion—many times over. Dad believes that Mom learned her fierce determination and unquenchable desire to succeed from her humble beginnings. Somewhere in that little tomboy's head—she played sports with the neighborhood boys and usually bested them—there burned this desire to excel.

Each day as a child, Mom passed San Diego's University Heights public tennis courts en route to her favorite playground. She usually skipped by these three courts attached to the public playground, looking for the day's pick-up baseball game. One day, at age nine, for whatever reason, she lingered to watch a tennis match in progress.

After that, she became as much a permanent fixture at the University Heights courts as a tennis net. She would cling to the fence outside the three tennis courts and watch the play for hours.

To his eternal credit, Wilbur Folsom, the tennis professional at those local courts, noticed the little girl. In time, he gave her lessons in return for shagging balls during his regular lessons.

It wasn't long before he noticed something different about little Maureen. Her eagerness to learn and her burning desire to excel caught his attention.

Mom wrote about her immediate love for tennis and her resolve to be the best at it in *Forehand Drive*:

I would become a tennis star! There was no middle
ground; only the top would suffice. Thus, in the next two
months, I became Folsom's shadow, a whirling dervish
as a ball boy, the most eager pupil he ever had.

Soon, Mom was spending all of her spare time on the tennis
courts. But unlike a thousand and one other pint-sized tennis players across the country in those days, her determination and mental toughness meant that she was a great
proponent of practice from an early age.

"In time," Dad said, "she developed absolute determination as a personality trait in everything she did. She was
like a force of nature."

At age eleven, she reached the finals in her first tournament, a local 13-and-under competition in San Diego. She
was beaten 8–6, 6–2 by Anne Bissell—and vowed it would
never happen again.

"I was very disappointed at losing and knew right then
that someday I wanted to reach the top in the tennis field,"
she wrote in her book *Power Tennis* (first published in 1954
by A.S. Barnes & Co.). "From there on in, it has been work,
work, and more work with practice sessions beginning at
9:00 AM and winding up around dinnertime. To become at
all proficient in any field, *practice and determination are the only
ways to reach your goal.*"

But in the 1940s, tennis was a rich man (and woman's)
game. It was played by wealthy amateurs, tall, willowy and
elegant, amid splendid country clubs, deftly sending
right-hand shots over immaculate courts.

Mom was poor, short, and left-handed.

When Folsom mentioned to Mom that the best tennis
players in the world were right-handed, Mom immediately
switched from being a natural lefty, to a right-handed player
overnight. It is intriguing to think how much better Mom
could have been if she had kept her natural swing. Mom ate,
wrote and played other sports left-handed, but was determined to be a right hander in tennis if that would give her an

advantage. Nana told me that Mom practiced against the backboard for hours to strengthen her right arm.

Her work ethic became legendary among her peers. It fueled her will to succeed.

Did it cost her? Of course. In *Power Tennis*, she adds this poignant footnote:

"It wasn't always a bed of roses because I had to do a lot of good hard work and give up things I would have enjoyed doing in school. It meant missing my junior and senior proms because of tournaments. (At that time this seemed like a catastrophe.) I also had to skip a lot of parties and after-school activities because of practice sessions and early bedtime. But that really isn't very much to give up for something you love and enjoy doing, is it?"

Mom loved tennis so much she never stopped learning, never stopped trying to improve, even after it became obvious that there were no women's tennis players in the world who could touch her in the early 1950s.

Alan Hoby, tennis correspondent for the English newspaper *Sunday Express*, had this to say in July 1953:

> . . . pace plus power is the Connolly key weapon. Sizzling winners which screamed to the line, vicious forehand, stinging services, searing cross-court backhand—all came alike to Maureen. It was inhuman stuff . . . not a human being at all, but a clockwork doll, a relentless, ruthless machine who on this form would beat most of the men in this country, let alone the women.

Even so, shortly after her third Wimbledon victory in 1954, she told reporter Harry Cronin that she was never satisfied with her game:

"I have a lot more confidence in my volley now and I feel my service is better. It still needs improving, though. My swing is wrong. It's too jerky. I'm trying to correct it."

One of the areas where Mom felt she could improve her game was with the deceptively simple drop shot. When she identified it as a weakness, she writes that "I practiced hundreds of hours on the drop shot, and I believe I achieved deception."

From what I heard from Ben Press, Mom may have been too modest. Ben told me she spent *thousands* of hours practicing the drop shot—and every other shot in her repertoire.

"Maureen and I lived a few doors from each other," Ben said. "We grew up together, but I was a little older than she. I had hopes of being a good tennis player, but it didn't work out. Still, Maureen and I were at the courts early every morning to late at night."

In those days, Ben recalled, you had to reach a certain level of proficiency before someone would play you. And with a limited number of available courts, that meant you'd better be good when you got there or no one would play with you. As usual, that didn't stop Mom.

"Before she got so good," Ben recalled, "we had a wall on the courts where, by herself, she'd hit endless numbers of balls. There were only three courts and they were busy all the time after school with anybody with any capability at all. When she mastered the wall, then she joined us.

"But before all of that, my main memory is of Maureen endlessly hitting practice balls against the wall."

From there, Ben said Mom would practice with *anybody* who would play with her. After she improved, she in turn would play with anybody who asked to hit with her. Either way, she had a lot of practice.

"There was, at that particular point in her life," Ben said, "very little time during daylight hours when she *wasn't* on those courts.

"From her front door to a tennis court was only 30 yards, so her mother could keep an eye on her when she'd go out there, even when she was little. As she got better, she practiced even more. We played every day for years, even after she became famous."

When Mom began playing tournaments, Ben said she still returned to those same three public courts in San Diego and practiced at night. I always thought it had to do with a certain loyalty to those courts. But Ben said there was something more.

"The lights at those particular courts were strung from end to end," he said. "Each light had a little reflector—maybe five reflectors on the whole court—and one or two were always burned out.

"In the days leading up to a tournament, we'd go up and hit at night—even though it meant we were virtually playing in the dark. The point is that we learned to watch the ball so carefully playing under those inadequate lights that by the time we got to the tournaments, the ball looked like a big balloon!"

Now, that's someone who loves tennis! Tennis enabled a little freckle-faced Irish girl to compete in some of the greatest championship games in the world. Tennis took Mom around the world. She got to see the coronation of Queen Elizabeth II, meet with the Pope, and go to exciting places like Hawaii and Australia.

But if tennis was the engine that steamrolled her career forward, it was hard work and practice that served as the fuel for that powerful locomotive. I firmly believe that had Mom chosen golf or equestrian sports or anything else where you can get better with practice, she would have excelled in them as well. The key is to practice *and to keep on practicing.*

She once said, "One thing about tennis—you can never stop learning. Each match played will find different shots skimming over the net toward you and each ball calls for a different type of answer."

Mom knew that excellence in all things is only obtained through practice and dedication. She worked as hard at being a tremendous wife and mom as she did at becoming a great tennis player.

The London Times once wrote about Mom, "Her rise to the top appeared meteoric, but it was the result of sheer hard work and intensity that has seldom been equaled in the game."

There is a parable about a famous violinist who once enthralled an audience at Carnegie Hall. Afterwards, a well-known society matron rushed forward and gushed, "I am in awe of your genius. I would give anything to play that well!"

And the virtuoso is said to have responded, "Anything? Would you have given yourself to eight hours of practice a day for the past thirty years as I have?"

Excellence is achieved only through practice.

Dad said that it was that attribute that she looked for in young tennis players as well:

"We always had two or three up-and-coming young tennis talents staying with us at the house so she could work with them. She preferred young people who *really* wanted to be good, not just youngsters who already were champions. She looked for youngsters who *wanted* to do better."

Mom believed that the eagerness to practice was perhaps *the* primary prerequisite for champions. There is a revealing quote tucked away in an interview she did with a Dallas newspaper in 1964. Mom and the reporter were watching a group of talented young tennis players. She turned to the reporter and said, "These kids want to work. That's so important. I look first for eagerness, then for a fluid stroke. Eagerness makes you work hard and hard work overcomes a lot of things which don't come naturally."

In a tribute to Mom, *The London Times* remembered her single-minded work ethic:

> Her practice sessions were prodigious feats of concentration. On a hot and humid day at Forest Hills, she is remembered as having taken on several practice opponents one after the other, reducing them all to a state of exhaustion with a stream of accurate drives and volleys before she was satisfied with her play.

Put another way, do you remember this little ditty from your grade school days? "Good, better, best. Never let it rest. Until your good is better. And your better best." If it is worth doing, it is worth doing well.

Practice makes champions. There are no short cuts.

Mom was living proof.

6

Lesson Three

Invest in People's Lives

Make a difference in the lives of people. Mom lived this principle every day of her life. Her words, her life practically shouted: invest in people's lives. Be generous. Spend time with others. Be "other-focused," not "self-focused."

Perhaps one of the most inspiring and endearing stories about my mother was the day that the doctors told her that her cancer was terminal. This followed, you may remember, a week of grueling, exhausting tests at Memorial Sloan-Kettering Cancer Center. At the end of the week, her doctors sat Mom and Dad down and told them that their worst fears had been realized. Mom's cancer was terminal. She had had her "best days." It was just a matter of time.

At that moment, Mom looked up at the clock on the wall and said, "Oh my, it's ten to six."

Dad and the doctors looked up with tears in their eyes—a little confused—and Dad said, "Yes Mosey, it's ten of six."

She said, "The three of you stay here, I've got to go. I met an older lady earlier this week and she's having cataract surgery tomorrow. Her family isn't here and she has no one. I told her that I had a doctor's appointment this afternoon but that I would visit her right after it was finished. I've got to go cheer her up because she's so scared about this cataract surgery. I've got to be there for her."

Dad said he'd never forget the sight of Mom, walking down the hospital corridor in her pink bathrobe and pink slippers, going down the hall to cheer another person up, just moments after having been given a death sentence.

"One of the doctors turned to me," Dad recalled, "and said, 'I've been in this business a long time and I've helped a lot of people, but I've never met someone as brave and as positive as Maureen.'"

Back in the '50s, the social ill that grabbed all the headlines was juvenile delinquency. What Mom wanted to do after her accident in 1954 was take kids out of the juvenile courts and put them on the tennis courts, figuratively speaking. An old scrapbook I have has photo after photo of Mom working with kids of all races—and this is 1959!—in neighborhood parks and centers. Since tennis had been a way for her to maximize the talents God had given her, she wanted to give something back to her beloved sport.

Ben Press said that even though she became an instant celebrity after she won Wimbledon the first time in 1952, she was never too busy to talk to people.

"She treated people with respect," Ben said, "no matter what they said or did. Back in those days, the reporters assigned to writing about tennis weren't always experts in the sport. It didn't matter to Maureen. In the press room after a big match, she patiently answered every question, no matter how inappropriate or mindless. Whatever the question, she never turned anyone away."

But Ben's most vivid memory of how Mom invested in the lives of others doesn't have to do with a reporter or a charity tournament. It has to do with a little girl with stars in her eyes.

"I had a student who was a great fan of Maureen's," Ben recalled. "One day, after Maureen had moved away, she returned to San Diego to play an exhibition match. This little girl asked me, 'Do you think Miss Connolly would hit with me? Maybe even watch me play and give me a few pointers?'

"I said I'd see what I could do. I happened to pick Maureen up at the airport and asked her and—of course—she said yes. I took her to the court and my awe-struck little student got to rally awhile with Maureen.

"Maureen then graciously said, 'I haven't been playing as much lately, so my timing is a bit off. Why don't I sit down and rest and watch you hit with Ben?' So we did. Maureen watched and gave her some suggestions. She never appeared to be in a hurry. She took the time to be friendly. Afterwards, I took her to her exhibition. It wasn't much to Maureen, but it meant everything to my student. She went on to be a nationally ranked junior woman. In part, I think, because of Maureen.

"Why was she like this? I believe Maureen always remembered what it was like growing up and not having much. *She never forgot how people helped her.*"

That was due, in part, to the fact that Mom's childhood had been unusually difficult. She was reared by a single mom and her great aunt. Money was scarce in their household and opportunities were slim. But my Nana persevered.

Even today Nana remains vivid in my memory. She once had dreams of being a concert pianist, but she was a small woman with smaller hands that could not span an octave. Consequently, Nana played the piano in San Diego-area music groups and the organ at five different churches on Sundays. When Mom wanted to take ballet lessons, they couldn't afford the cost. So Nana played the piano at the lessons in exchange for Mom's lesson fees. Mom later attributed her success on the tennis court, in part, to those ballet lessons.

Ben Press said the money available to promising young tennis players wasn't like it is now, but Southern California during that particular era was the tennis pipeline for the whole world.

"Perry T. Jones and the Southern California Tennis Association ran the show," Ben said. "That meant when it became obvious that Maureen was a really promising player, Perry made sure she had some financial support—enough to sustain her, anyway. It wasn't long before Wilson Sporting Goods gave her tennis rackets and balls. It made a difference when you could practice with new balls—they were such a rarity back then. It wasn't much, but things like that made the struggle a whole lot less.

"Maureen never forgot this and always tried to give something back."

Mom invested freely in the lives of others. When she became champion, Mom remembered her roots. She wanted to return something back to the sport that had given her so much. That's how the Maureen Connolly Brinker Tennis Foundation was founded with Nancy Jeffett:

"When Cindy and Brenda were still little, the Brinkers moved to Dallas," Nancy recalled. "I was the chairman of the Texas Tennis Association's junior development program at the time. Maureen and I had been friends since our tennis playing days. So, once she came to Dallas, we renewed our friendship."

It wasn't long before Mom and Nancy began to organize tennis-related activities for children, including tennis clinics, programs, and lessons. Soon, Nancy focused on the administrative work, while Mom gravitated naturally towards the teaching.

"We need a year-round program for the young players in Texas," Mom told *The Dallas Times Herald* in April 1966. "Financial support is necessary.

"I will do some touring, giving talks on tennis and instructions at high schools and playgrounds. I think all this will help also in combating juvenile delinquency."

Nancy said it wasn't long before their scope became a little more ambitious.

"We started raising a little money to support it," she said, "especially through mixed doubles tournaments and other charity events."

"Maureen grew up in a real tennis mecca, Southern California, and when she arrived in Dallas she could see that there was so much to do in Texas to motivate and encourage youngsters in tennis. She always said she'd had such an exciting and full life because of her tennis and that she wanted to give back to others. Both of us did. We both wanted to do something for young people in the tennis world. So we put our heads together and we envisioned ways we could strengthen the tennis programs, send players off to tournaments, provide clinics—whatever we could to make a mark on junior tennis."

This informal arrangement lasted for quite a while before Mom and Nancy decided to incorporate and create the Maureen Connolly Brinker Tennis Foundation.

And since holding clinics, sending promising young players to national championships and supporting young people was costing a lot of money, the next logical step was to get involved with fundraising.

"But Maureen's health continued to fail," Nancy said. "We incorporated the Maureen Connolly Brinker Tennis Foundation with fifty dollars in the bank just before she died. She inspired me to carry on the foundation and I've had a real rich thirty-something years furthering all the things she and I initially talked about.

"Eventually, after Maureen's passing, we developed the Virginia Slims of Dallas tournament, which would be our main fundraiser for years. This was all part of her dream."

The foundation was Mom's way of helping others. Initially, it was designed just for girls as a way of supporting promising juniors who couldn't afford the lessons, travel, lodging, and food expenses necessary to compete in the top-notch tournaments. Eventually, the foundation supported boys' tennis activities and tournaments as well, but the original mission remains the same today—furthering

junior tennis development worldwide. The foundation continues to give travel grants and sportsmanship awards. It is
one of the largest private tennis foundations of its kind in
the world.

Mom's accomplishments are in all the sports history
books. She's a legend in tennis. She was a world champion
twice over. But to Brenda and me, Mom's greatest contribu-
tions were not on the green pitch at Wimbledon, they were
off the tennis court. It's what she did by giving back to the
sport that, we believe, is her greatest contribution. The lives
that have been touched by the Maureen Connolly Brinker
Tennis Foundation and her personal commitment to tennis
will be one of her lasting legacies.

Among the international events sponsored by the foundation is a tournament that features the top 19-and-under
girls in the United States versus the top 19-and-under girls
in Great Britain. The tournament site alternates each year
between the two countries. Brenda participates annually,
and I am able to go to the tournaments when they are held in
the United States.

Tennis stars like Zina Garrison, Chris Evert, Pam
Shriver, and Tracy Austin are all past participants in programs sponsored by the foundation. And all of them have
been publicly bold, gracious and appreciative in acknowl-
edging their involvement with the foundation.

And it all started because one of Mom's core values was
to invest in other people.

Reverend Elliott Greene, an anointed assistant minister
in discipleship and pastoral care at our church in Dallas and
a beloved friend of Bob's and mine, once said to me that it is
not important if you have the capabilities to lead. What *is*
important is if you are *worthy* to be followed.

"The ingredients of worthiness are patience, love,
integrity, and humility," Reverend Greene says.

In my experience of dealing with people, I have
observed that each individual has two distinct sides to their
personalities—their "doing" side and their "is" side. A

person's total composite has both of these personality traits intertwined, yet very independent of each other. The achievements and accomplishments of a person would be classified as his/her active or "doing" side. This is an external feature. The character, values and motives of that same individual would be classified as who that person "is." It is an internal barometer of his/her personality. Yet, a person can be a highly skilled and accomplished leader whose internal values bear witness to a total deficiency of character and integrity.

We see examples of this throughout history. Adolf Hitler was capable of leading but was he worthy of being followed? I think not! It is important to really evaluate, beyond just a publicized achievement, the true essence of a person. Are others worthy to be followed? Are we ourselves worthy to be followed?

How does Little Mo rate in this litmus test? Mom's life certainly achieved stellar status as the best in the world at what she did. She also nobly conducted her life in a way that admirably gave back to others. Mom was a role model whose brief life was marked by integrity, humility, and an "other-focused" mentality. In short, her personal and professional lifework garnered respect and was worthy to be followed.

One of my favorite quotes says, "All that is necessary for the forces of evil to win the world is for enough good people to do nothing."

It just takes one visionary with one good idea, one crusader to begin a movement and others will follow. Conversely, when good ideas are not put into motion, and people of noble character do not act, great things do not happen and bad things can prosper. I wonder how many extraordinary crusades, brilliant ideas or innovative breakthroughs have not seen daylight because there was no investment of time, resources, energy, and confidence in seeing them through. I wonder if perhaps there might already have been a cure for ovarian cancer if a researcher had followed through on his/her hunch.

Both my parents had servant's hearts. Both thought that "giving back" was a celebrated, yet mandatory, duty, a sacred responsibility. They didn't just talk about doing good things—*they acted.*

I remember very vividly one day when my dad's mother, Dad, and I were talking together. Grandma had just asked Dad, "Norman, what have you been up to lately?"

Dad began to talk in very excited tones about the successes he was experiencing at Steak & Ale and about the chain's upcoming expansion. He was really fired up!

My grandmother interrupted Dad in the middle of his sentence (she was the only person in the world who would dare do that!) and said in her schoolteacher voice, "Norman, I am not talking about *those* things. I am talking about what is *really* important! I am talking about what have you been doing for your community, your country, your church?"

She was a no-nonsense lady. But I have always remembered her message. Brenda's and my legacy of volunteerism actually started many generations ago.

Another hero of mine, Traci Taylor, taught me about being "other-focused."

At age six, Traci was diagnosed with acute myeloid leukemia. Traci became one of Wipe Out Kids' Cancer's ambassadors at age eight. Traci's prognosis wasn't good and doctors gave her little hope of survival. But her prognosis didn't take into account the tenacious strength of her spirit and her uncommon zest for life.

Her epic struggle with cancer left her with a burning desire to do something for the other pediatric cancer patients who were receiving weekly chemotherapy treatments at the same hospital where she was receiving her treatments. Traci asked her father and brother to build her a train. She solicited cash and in-kind donations from businesses and retailers. With the money, she bought craft items and toys. Each

Thursday for years when she was receiving her treatments, she filled her train with these items and distributed them free of charge to her fellow patients. Long after she stopped receiving her treatments, she continued to take her train to the hospital and deliver complimentary toys to the cancer patients. No one knows how many lives she brightened.

Traci was honored by President George H. Bush at the White House for her outstanding commitment to others. She also received the Maxwell House Hero Award for Community Leadership.

Sadly, Traci died in 2000 at age nineteen, leaving a legacy of activism and hope to a generation of sick children. One beautiful young woman, not even twenty, investing in the lives of others, made a difference. One dreamer, one visionary, one person who saw beyond the first step and took it, to make a difference. One person, fallible and ordinary, can make such a difference.

How much of a difference? We won't know in this lifetime. But our calling is to *do*. We'll let Someone Else tabulate results down the road.

Grief is not a new emotion. Activism is not a new phenomenon. But I have found that when you marry the two and become "other-focused," the burden of that grief can be lifted and true healing can begin to take place.

The Bible says, "To whom much is given, much is required." That verse motivates me daily.

What am *I* doing for others? What are *you* doing for others?

I am reminded of a beautiful quote by Margaret Mead: "Never doubt that a small group of thoughtful, committed citizens can change the world. Indeed, it's the only thing that ever has."

And today is a *great* day to get started.

7

Lesson Four

Maximize Each Day

Mom died at age thirty-four. During the year I turned thirty-four, I calculated the exact minute that I was older than my mom. That was a sobering point in my life. How very young she was when death claimed her. At that point, I'd only been married a year. At that same point in her life, Mom had been married fourteen years, had a twelve- and a ten-year-old, had been the third most publicized woman in the world (in the early 1950s), and had dominated the sport of tennis. She accomplished so much in such a cruelly short life span.

Little Mo, the made-for-TV movie about Mom's life, was previewed by saying, "This is about a little girl in a hurry." Perhaps Mom knew—on some subconscious, intuitive level—that she only had a short window of time on earth. Perhaps that filled her with an unspoken sense of urgency in her life.

Her untimely death at thirty-four has made me highly sensitive to the concept of maximizing each day, of living each day to the fullest. I find it very difficult to ever just "waste time."

That urgency has impacted me in another significant way. I don't take *any* relationships for granted. When Bob and I kiss goodbye in the morning, I am acutely aware that this could possibly be our last embrace. Having already lost a loved one, I know we cannot just assume that we have tonight, much less tomorrow. Nobody knows the time of their homecoming.

And while I'm not obsessed with thoughts of how fragile life is, I am keenly aware of that eternal truth. Even with William. Every minute, I want to just squeeze him so tightly, because I am not guaranteed tomorrow.

Friends are always telling me to slow down. They're forever sending me thoughtful notes that say things like, "When things slow down for you (ha ha!) . . .". But I just can't seem to put it in neutral because I've got so many irons in the fire. I just can't because I know how quickly that fire burns out.

As I've grown and matured, I now look back on Mom's life and see something entirely different. Even though she lived such a short life, her time was up—right on schedule, according to plan. Thirty-four years and a handful of days. As painful as that was—and still is—she played hard and when the trumpet sounded at the end of the game, she had finished in victory. No regrets—a short lifetime of victories—and then her time was up.

Our dear pastor Elliott Greene said he would revise the popular quote "Live each day as though it were your last" to read "Live each day as though it were your best."

"Living each day as though it were your last promotes desperation," he said. "Living each day as though it were your best promotes excellence. A person should not be enslaved to compulsion."

An individual should do his/her very best in maximizing the gifts and talents he/she has been given.

Truly, Mom lived each day as though it were her very best. When the sun set on her final day, she could have no regrets. Excellence, not compulsion, had been her standard.

None of us knows when our time is up. And if we don't know that one fundamental fact, then we should feel almost honor-bound not to waste a single precious day.

My mom was always proactive. Her life buzzed with activity, it crackled with involvement, it burned with life. It was almost like you could see the dust trailing behind her. She was always productive. And yet, she was very balanced, focused and deliberate in her priorities—especially to her family.

Dad said it was a revelation living with someone with that kind of life-force:

"She exemplified the concept of 'maximize each day.' When she worked for Wilson Sporting Goods in an advisory position, for instance, she gave clinics around the country. And whenever she left home, she was totally organized. She knew exactly what she was doing, where she was doing it, whom she was seeing—and when. Every single time.

"Even when we'd go on vacation, she had read everything in advance and was so knowledgeable about what we were seeing. She'd say, 'Here's what happened in this house in 1650.' Just looking at buildings isn't always all that interesting. But she made history come alive—because she knew it and loved it. She absolutely had it all down pat."

Ben Press and Mom played regularly together even after her accident whenever she was in San Diego. But age and retirement didn't change Mom one bit!

"I'll bet we played together five hundred times," Ben recalled, "and if she wasn't having as good a day as she wanted and I'd ease off a little bit, she'd always detect it. She'd shout across the court, 'Don't you *dare* let up on me, Ben. Don't you dare.' She didn't want me to play anything but all out.

"She wanted to play like she lived—all out."

Mom thrived on productive activity and—perhaps most amazingly of all—she also thrived on balance.

Somehow Mom managed to create a sense of balance in her life. She was a working mother. She wrote articles in various tennis magazines, she commentated at Wimbledon, she coached promising young players, she held tennis clinics, she gave tennis lessons. At the same time, she read voraciously—how she loved to read. She was a room mother while Brenda and I were in school. She took college courses. She always had a project going on around the house. She was an adoring, nurturing wife and mother *and* she helped Dad start his business. Oh, and I almost forgot, she also happened to have her own autographed line of tennis rackets as a member of the Wilson Sporting Goods Advisory Board. I once calculated that she held four full-time jobs!

Dad said that level of involvement spilled over into every facet of Mom's life.

"She displayed that same absolute determination as a wife and mom," he said. "She played tennis with Cindy, rode with Brenda, and supported me in polo.

"When I had Brink's Coffee Shop in Dallas, then opened Steak & Ale in 1966, I almost quit polo—it was just too much of a time commitment. She said, 'No, no, no. I'll exercise the horses. I'll have them ready when it's time to play.' And she did. She threw herself into polo, galloping the ponies, getting everything ready for me when polo matches would roll around."

"Maureen gave 100 percent of herself to her children, to her husband," Nancy Jeffett said. "Norman was building a business at the time and she encouraged him in everything he did. She never demanded anything of anybody. She always said, 'I'm just fine. You go on and do what you need to do.' She had the most unbelievable upbeat attitude.

"It was easy to see why she was a champion on the tennis courts—she was such a champion in every other aspect of her life."

Mom was always healthy in terms of her balance. And that's what I want for my life—balance and productivity. I've got the proactive and productive part down, but the balance part is a daily challenge.

It's not easy—as every mom knows.

Reverend Greene compares frenzied activity to being on a treadmill. You're working hard, sweating and groaning. This activity level has all the outward appearance of progress—but you're not actually moving forward at all. You're running in the same place.

"A treadmill gives you the reality of motion with the illusion of progress," Reverend Greene said. "It's like a dog

Top—Maureen, Brenda
(age 7), Cindy (age 9), and
Norman in December
1966.

Right—Little Mo as Little
Mom with toddler Cindy
and infant Brenda.

At age 6, Cindy takes her first tennis lesson from her mother.

Cindy (age 11), Norman, Maureen, and Brenda (age 9) at home for Christmas in 1968. This was the last family photograph taken before Maureen died in June 1969.

At age 12, Cindy seriously began playing tennis.

Cindy practicing her serve.

Top—Norman and Cindy presenting the first Maureen Connolly Brinker Outstanding Junior Girl Award to Eliza Pande in August 1969. Today, this is the most distinguished award presented in junior girls' tennis.

Left—Cindy, at age 14, was ranked first in Texas and in the top ten in the United States in her age division.

Cindy and Bob on their wedding day, February 24, 1990.
Photo by Tom Robertson.

Cindy is joined by Addison, Texas Mayor Scott Wheeler, Wipe Out Kids' Cancer Executive Director Paige McDaniel, and the 2000 Wipe Out Kids' Cancer ambassadors at a major fund raiser in Addison

Cindy, William (age 5), and Bob at Christmas 2000.
Photo by James M. Innes

William is a little prayer warrior.
Photo by James M. Innes

running after its tail. You are plenty busy but you are not going anywhere."

Personally, I have seen how being busy can steer me away from balance. My plate is full, my calendar is booked, my life is exciting. Idleness is a foreign word. But I can easily lose my balance on that fast treadmill. My footing can become unstable and the fall is hard. Mom's pace was always even, steady and consistent. She never seemed to break a sweat! I admire her so much for keeping her priorities intact and keeping her life in balance.

I've often wondered how Mom kept it all together— humility in spite of her fame, balance in the wake of the tremendous demands on her life and wisdom in the midst of all of her personal and professional decisions.

I recently found another interesting and revealing interview with Mom published in *The Denver Post* in the early 1960s. It gave me a renewed appreciation of how she always kept a level head about her life:

> I'm Mrs. Norman Brinker now. Nobody recognizes me anymore and I'm glad of it.
>
> You have to keep things in proper perspective. My life was all tennis when I was a kid and that was wonderful— how else could any teenager have traveled the world in style as I did? But then came the time to quit and get married and I did.
>
> Now, there's nothing sadder to me than athletes who don't quit at the peak and you watch them going downhill. It's all such a false glamour. But what I have is real.

And that was the way Mom wanted it. Her first love was her family; her tennis career was a distant second.

When Mom passed away, Dad called a meeting of the three of us to decide what was to be on her tombstone. A thirty-eight-year-old husband and his twelve-year-old and ten-year-old daughters were to sum up the life of this gifted woman who had served as the nucleus of their lives. It was a challenging task. After tears and lots of tender words, we came up with a beautiful description of Mom. Her tomb-stone has a set of crossed tennis rackets at the top. It reads:

Maureen Connolly Brinker

1934–1969

A Gallant Lady

Wife

Mother

Champion

I think Mom would have been very happy with that. I suspect that was the key to her remarkable balance. She had her priorities right. Once you know what's really important and tend to that aspect of your life first, everything else seems to fall into place on its own.

One day, decades ago, I forgot my lunch in the third grade. At the time, Janet Barnes, my teacher, had not had a chance to meet Mom because I had just enrolled in a new school in the middle of the school year due to our move to a new home. Miss Barnes knew that I was Little Mo's daughter.

Later that morning, Mom knocked lightly on the door to my classroom, lunch sack in hand.

Years later, Miss Barnes told me, "I glanced over to the door and there stands Little Mo, this celebrated person who I had read about and followed and idolized growing up. Even though I had never met her, I felt like I knew her and all the things she had done. But here she stood at my door, not as a tennis star, but as a concerned mother bringing her child her forgotten lunch sack.

"'Miss Barnes,' she said, 'I am so sorry. Please forgive me for interrupting your class. I am Cindy's mom, and I am bringing her lunch, which she forgot this morning. I didn't want her to go hungry. I'm so sorry to disturb you.'"

Just an ordinary Mom. Which is what she was—except she also happened to have been the best tennis player in the world.

Miss Barnes was so touched because—as she told me later—Mom had been her hero. And here was Little Mo profusely apologizing to her! Not as Little Mo, but as a mother.

As Mrs. Norman Brinker, the mother of Cindy, who had left her lunch.

Mom knew better than most that life is so transient. You may be on the top today but that might not be where you are tomorrow. So many people in the public eye don't seem to get the message. You have a window of time—some say it's just fifteen minutes—of fame. But when you start beginning to believe your own press, you become vulnerable to arrogance and pride. You become immune to humility.

Mistakes are necessary because they are the classroom of humility. A lot of humility education comes through learning from your mistakes. When we say that we don't make mistakes any more, *that's* when reality blindsides us. When we refuse to admit our mistakes—or blame them on someone else—that's the perfect breeding ground for arrogance.

You're never too old to stop learning. That's a life's work.

You're never too young to appreciate the day, to maximize the time you have. You might not have tomorrow.

I am reminded of this each year when I get a new calendar and start reviewing important dates for the upcoming year. Typically, when most people get a new calendar, they go to important birthdays and anniversaries in the new year and review those days. It's human nature to highlight special moments and celebrations in the year to come.

But for years in my teens, early twenties and even into my late twenties, when I got a new calendar, I always flipped first to the day Mom died, June 21, and put a big, black "X" through it. For years, Mom's loss was so sorrowful to me that it was like I was trying to obliterate that day, to forget it entirely. Symbolically, I was attempting to make June 21 disappear. I despised that day.

At age nineteen, in a journal entry on June 21, 1976, at 4:10 p.m., I wrote these words while sitting by her grave at Sparkman-Hillcrest:

> How I have dreaded this day. The memory of its significance fills my heart with the greatest sadness. It seems as if it would get easier to accept Mom's death, but each

year, I feel more pain at her loss . . . with each approach-
ing year, I realize how much I miss her, and the great
potential we would have had in talking and rap sessions.
She was so wise!

How painful it is reading that entry. The depth of my grief
on Mom's death anniversary is overwhelming. June 21 was a
very dark day for me for years and years.

Today, when I get that new calendar, my ritual has
changed slightly. I turn to Bob's, William's, Dad's, Brenda's,
Katina's, and my birthday and Bob's and my anniversary.
But then, when I finish with this ritual, I automatically go to
June 21 and stare at that date—with years of reflection rac-
ing through my mind in a matter of seconds.

I don't draw an "X" through that date anymore, but I still
wish with all of my heart that it wasn't there. It represents the
day a precious life ended so prematurely. It represents a day
that radically and forever impacted three other lives.

With the uncertainty of a new dawn appearing, it's never
too late to say "Thank you," "I love you" or "I'm sorry."
These are treasured words that will forever haunt you if the
deserving recipient never gets to hear them.

Mom always honored Dad in how she treated him, how
she spoke to him. And throughout our too-short time together,
I always heard her saying "thank you," "please," "I love you." I
mean, over and over and over again. It's never too late.

Reconcile your relationships. Now is not soon enough.

Mom faltered once in an important relationship. But it
was an incident that saddened her throughout her life.

Mom had a falling out with her great coach Teach
Tennant. During a tournament in England just prior to
Mom's first quest for a Wimbledon title in 1952, Mom accidentally forgot to put on her sweater after finishing a match
in the cool, damp English weather.

Her shoulder got chilled and she contracted fibrositis—a congested shoulder condition. When you're really hot and you've exerted yourself, Mom taught me to always put on a wrap so you don't cool down too fast. But this time she forgot to put on her sweater because she was signing autographs.

When Mom reported her sore shoulder to Teach, Teach thought it was a torn muscle. She withdrew Mom from Wimbledon and told the press that Little Mo had a torn shoulder muscle.

Mom was flabbergasted. In those days, coaches spoke for you. There was no such thing as players calling their own press conferences. Mom immediately met with Teach privately.

"Why did you do this?" she asked.

"Maureen, I don't want you to play Wimbledon because if you play with that torn shoulder, you'll ruin yourself," Teach said. "You'll never be able to play again."

Mom said, "No, it couldn't be a torn shoulder because even though I can't serve or hit an overhead, I can still hit a forehand and a backhand. I can volley. If it was a torn shoulder, it would affect all of my strokes."

But Teach was from the old school and would hear no arguments from her prize student.

"No," she said, "it's a torn shoulder. I've already withdrawn you."

But mom got a second opinion from a physician, and he said it was not a torn shoulder.

"You've got fibrositis," he said. "You should be able to play without any damage. We can treat you every day before your matches."

But when Mom told Teach, she was livid.

"Doctors just tell you what you want to hear," she raged. "I've withdrawn you from Wimbledon and if you play . . . .".

It wasn't a particularly subtle threat. But Mom knew her own body, she knew what she was capable of and playing would not irreparably damage her shoulder. Besides, playing at Wimbledon had always been her dream and she had worked so hard to get to this point.

So, for the first time in Wimbledon history, Mom called a press conference. No player had ever done this before. The press adored Mom, so when Little Mo spoke, everybody came running.

Mom stood before the press corps of England and said, "I am playing Wimbledon. I'm not withdrawing."

Mom played Wimbledon and won. It was, indeed, fibrositis. But that incident created a severance between player and coach.

They never spoke again. Still, all her life, Mom regretted the incident and its outcome. In *Forehand Drive*, Mom wrote, "Our quarrel was bitter, leaving scars which have never healed."

She repeatedly told me in later years, "I'll talk to Teach. I need to visit with her. We'll reconcile. She was so special to me."

But for whatever reason, she never did it.

And Teach never contacted Mom. Perhaps she thought that since Mom was indebted to her for her success that Mom should be the one to make the first move. Perhaps Mom thought that since Teach was the adult, and because she had resurrected Teach's career, that Teach ought to be the one to call first.

Both of them thought, "I'll do it someday," but "someday" never came. Mom died before they reconciled.

In 1994, I was in California implementing a client promotion. The event was in Costa Mesa, right outside of San Diego. I knew that Teach once lived in the area. So I asked someone who was active in the tennis scene, "Is Teach Tennant still alive?"

The last I had heard was that she'd been partially blinded through cataracts and, to be honest, I wasn't sure she was still alive.

My friend said, "Teach is still alive but her eyesight is failing. She's very old and in the twilight of her life, but she's alive."

I got Teach's phone number and I called her. I was as nervous as a young girl called into the principal's office. I imagine Mom would have been just as nervous.

A feeble voice answered, "Hello?"

I said, "Teach?"—because that's how I'd known her.

There was a pause. "Yes?"

"Teach, you don't know me but my name is Cindy Brinker Simmons. You knew my mom, Maureen 'Little Mo' Connolly."

There was another pause on the line, a longer one, but I stumbled ahead anyhow.

"Teach, I want you to know that my Mom loved you. She always gave you credit for her career. She regretted deeply that she never reconciled with you after your split. She respected you so much." I blurted all of this out in a rush.

Still nothing.

"Teach, did you know that Mom died?"

At last, Teach spoke. "Yes, Cindy, I knew she died. I was so sad, it broke my heart."

"Teach, the thing that broke Mom's heart was that she never reconciled with you. That burdened her and was on her heart her entire life. So I'm calling and asking for forgiveness for my mom, and to let you know how much you meant to her."

On the other end of the phone, I could hear Teach crying softly.

She said, "It has been one of the greatest heartbreaks in my life that we never reconciled. Your mom was a great champion."

After that, we had a lovely chat. We both cried during the conversation. When it was over, I felt blessed that I had been able to do that for my mom.

But those kinds of reconciliations don't always happen. They're not always even possible. I realized right then and there that I *cannot* take any unresolved issues or relationships to my grave.

Today is the day to tell your loved ones that you love them.

Today is the day to seek forgiveness or write that thank you note you've put off so long.

Today is the day to kiss your child one more time.

Why?

Because you never know if you will experience the dawn tomorrow.

Maximize each day.

You can say, "I'll get to that."

You can have every intention of doing the right thing, of getting back in good graces. But that day might not ever come.

Through Mom's relationship with Teach Tennant, I learned that it's important to ask for forgiveness *now*. Don't wait!

Holding grudges can cripple the heart with bitterness and anger. Even if a person does not ask for forgiveness, we need to forgive him or her for the offense so that we do not harbor ill-will, hatred, or bitterness.

Maximize each day. Praise God. Live each day as though it were your best. Greet each day with a smile in your heart. Hug your loved ones. Hug them again. Forgive others. Don't let another hour go by without reconciling a relationship.

Your life will be changed.

Lesson Five

The Awesome Power of Love and Touch

I learned so much from watching Mom and Dad. They were always hugging and touching. Brenda and I felt the love of Mom and Dad filter down to us. The greatest gift a father can give his children is to love his wife. The greatest gift a mother can give her children is to love her husband. Brenda and I were so secure in our love because of the love our parents had for each other.

Growing up, my family was big into hugs. Mom hugged Dad, Dad hugged Brenda, Mom hugged me, and yes—Brenda and I hugged. It was one big "hug-in." All my life, I have treasured the closeness of a hug.

Today, William feels the security of our hugs. We often engage in "family hugs" where all three of us will embrace in a big hug. William loves to initiate them: "Let's have a family hug." This bonds us as a family.

When William says, "Hug me real tight," he grabs one of us around the neck, squeezes and showers us with kisses. He needs hugs. We all do.

The kiss is also important to William at this age—although I understand that once he turns into a teenager we need to be careful! But for now, he still says just before he goes to bed, "Mommy, kiss me very gently all over." Or, he will say, "Kiss me a lot of times." So I give him soft kisses all over his face. There is a "love language" between us that jells our relationship.

This sort of jelling also needs a verbal language. We constantly say things to William like, "I choose you," "You are splendid," and "You are special." He loves hearing those words. In these repeated phrases, we are building self-esteem, love, and unity as a family. William flashes a big grin every time we give those "verbal hugs."

As I was growing up, my dad would come into my room every morning and say, "Good morning, sunshine." I knew I was loved.

Mom and Dad had one of those fairy-tale romances you read about. After winning her first Wimbledon, the citizens of San Diego wanted to give their "Little Mo" a car in appreciation of her remarkable victory, but she said she'd prefer a horse. It was love at first sight between Colonel Merry Boy and Mom.

Concurrently, Dad was stationed in the Navy, based in the San Diego area and training for the 1952 Olympic equestrian team. Both Mom and Dad chose the same stables.

Mom wrote a regular column for *The San Diego Union*, "Letter from Li'l Mo." Her uncle had arranged a meeting between Mom and Dad, and Mom decided to do a story on this handsome Olympian for her column. Dad quickly agreed.

The first question Mom asked (of course!) was, "Are you married?" Dad's response was, "No, and dedicated to staying that way!"

Not to be sidelined, Mom called him back after this first interview and said she still had some more questions to ask him for her column. He answered them and then asked *her* out.

And what to do on their first date? Play a friendly game of tennis! Honestly, my Dad is a very smart man. However, I would not put this on the top ten list of the most intelligent things he has ever done!

To his credit, Dad was a great athlete and a fairly good tennis player. But Mom was the world champion female player. She was merciless.

"Maureen did not ease up on me at all," Dad laughed. "She'd use a drop shot, a lob, and then she'd slam one by me. Actually, she ran me all over the court. We had been playing about thirty minutes when I walked over to pick up a ball by the fence. Because the lights were shining brightly we couldn't see out—and when I got to the fence, I noticed there were about fifteen people watching. One kid had his fingers through the fence and, as I leaned over to pick up the ball, he said, 'Boy, mister, do we feel sorry for you.'"

Dad was smitten. He never did come close to beating her in tennis, but he eventually won the "love match"— despite being transferred around the country with the Navy and his marathon Olympic practice sessions *and* her grueling travel schedule. Dad had pursued the girl they were calling "America's Sweetheart" with the same determination he'd approached everything else in life.

When he finally met Nana to ask for Mom's hand in marriage, he'd left the Navy and was attending San Diego State University. Nana's first question—born out of a lifetime of poverty—was how he planned to support her.

"I'm going to sell cutlery door-to-door," Dad said, "just like in the Navy."

"How can you do that when people are now putting up 'No Solicitors' signs in their windows all over the neighborhood?"

"Oh," Dad said with a smile, "those are the houses I'm going to first. They'll be more receptive because other salesmen don't badger them."

Nana didn't have any choice—Dad won her over, too!

In 1955, Mom and Dad were married and were rarely apart after that. Such was the power of their love, their relationship, that right after I was born, Dad and Mom agreed to invest their life savings—$3,500—for Dad to become an investor in Jack-In-The-Box.

"Go for it," Mom said, "if that's what you want to do."

Mom was a team player. When Dad decided to leave Jack-in-the-Box to start a coffee shop in Dallas, it was Mom who helped plant the rock garden in the front of the restaurant. Money was tight so they did it together—one rock at a time.

And when Dad decided to create a brand new kind of restaurant chain—one modeled after the quintessential English tavern (this was when the movie *Tom Jones* was really big)—it was Mom who made sure the interiors were authentic while she was serving as a guest commentator at Wimbledon in 1962. Following her commentary duties at the end of the day, she would leave immediately, grab her drawing pad, and retire to the local English pubs to sketch the atmosphere.

She was often accompanied by her very close friend Mary Hare (the British champion who had hit with Mom when she was ten and to whom Mom had said, "One day I'm going to be the world's greatest tennis player.") and her husband Charles, a British tennis champion in his own right. Charles was worried about Mom's brutal schedule at Wimbledon, which included numerous guest appearances as well as commentating. But Mom would have none of it.

"I can't stop, Charlie," she said. "I've got to keep going. I only have three days left in England, and I want Norman to see these so we can design our restaurant as authentically as possible."

Dad was equally supportive in all of Mom's ventures.

He once told me that their relationship was magical: "Maureen was like the surprise in the Cracker Jacks box. I always looked forward to what she would do and say next."

They were partners in all things.

At one point in their marriage, in the midst of everything else they were doing, Mom and Dad operated a tennis club in San Diego with Ben Press. Sometimes running a business together isn't the easiest thing to do. But Ben said that throughout the years he saw Mom and Dad together, he only saw them behave towards each other in the most loving, affectionate way.

"I was with them frequently whenever they were in town," Ben said. "In all those years, I never saw them have a cross word.

"I've never been too good business-wise. I was more comfortable teaching and playing. Norm was the business mind. He was amazing. Norm ran the show, but he always deferred to Maureen. They were always so good with each other."

It was the power of their love, their relationship that enabled them to endure those dark days at Memorial Sloan-Kettering Cancer Center when she was so very, very sick. Through that whole ordeal, Dad was always there, touching her, holding her hand.

There is a power in love and touch. Perhaps you've heard of the ground-breaking studies by Spitz and Goldfarb in 1945. They studied clean, well-run orphanages where the children—especially the babies—received plenty of food and good medical care and yet inexplicably wasted away and died in chilling numbers.

What Spitz and Goldfarb discovered was that while the over-worked employees took care of most of the foundlings' physical needs, they simply didn't have time to cuddle and touch the babies. The babies were dying because the employees weren't meeting one of the most fundamental needs—that of touch and human contact. Spitz and Goldfarb reported that at least minimal physical stimulation (or "mothering") was essential to life itself.

We all crave it; it is mandatory to our well-being. To be touched and loved.

One hot afternoon when we were in Palm Desert, California, Mom was really struggling with pain and was in bed. She was almost in a trance-like state. I came in quietly, placed a cold washcloth on her forehead and moved that damp and cool washrag all around her face. Not saying a word, I just sat on the edge of her bed for over thirty minutes wiping her face, getting up only to refresh the washrag. Later that afternoon, Mom rallied and got out of bed. She thanked me so much and told Dad what a difference that had made in the way she felt.

The healing power of love and touch.

A dear friend of mine, Sherry O'Hearn, e-mails me encouraging stories and scriptures on a regular basis. One that has riveted my emotions is titled "A Box Full of Kisses."

> Some time ago, a man punished his three-year-old daughter for wasting a roll of gold wrapping paper. Money was tight and he was infuriated when the child tried to wrap a box to put under the Christmas tree. Nevertheless, the little girl brought the gift to her father the next morning and said, "This is for you, Daddy."
>
> He was embarrassed by his earlier reaction, but when he opened the box and found it was empty, he yelled at her, "Don't you know when you give someone a present, there's supposed to be something inside it?"
>
> The little girl looked up at him with tears in her eyes and said, "Oh Daddy, it's not empty, I blew kisses into the box. All for you."
>
> The father was crushed. He put his arms around his little girl, and he begged for her forgiveness.
>
> A car accident took the life of his little girl a short time later, and it is told that the man kept that gold box by his bed for many years. Whenever he was discouraged, he would take out an imaginary kiss and remember the love of the child who had put it there.

Whether visible or invisible, each of us has been given a gold container filled with love, hugs, and kisses from our children, family, friends, and God. There is no more precious possession.

Lesson Six

Be a Gracious Winner and Loser

Mom was a great believer in competition. She was a devout supporter of the benefits of competition afforded through any sport.
In 1962, she told *The Denver Post*:

> . . . I think children should learn to be competitive in something at an early age. There's no better lesson you can learn in life than losing, learning to grit your teeth and start again. It teaches you responsibility and gives you a goal.

Roy Edwards, in a 1970 article in *The Dallas Morning News* that ran prior to the Maureen Connolly Brinker Memorial Tournament, wrote about Mom's perspective on competition:

> To learn to accept a challenge, she would say, to learn to cope with success, to learn to bounce back from and overcome adversity, to learn how to raise your chin instead of dropping it on your chest—these are the benefits of competition.

And, of course, the twin consequences of competition are winning and losing.

It has always been important to be a gracious winner or loser. Both are difficult, but sometimes I think being a gracious winner is the harder of the two. How Mom handled winning—and she was basically unstoppable throughout her career—continues to be an inspiration to me.

Dad once told me, "I never saw your mom lose, but I know this: the few times in her past she did lose, she never blew up, she never threw a racket, she never hit a ball into the stands, and she never said anything to the linesman.

"She had such a sense of humility. She never bragged, she never cut in front of a line, she never seemed aware of her status."

To be a good loser, you have to be humble. To be a good winner, you have to be humble. Mom modeled both. Although winning and losing are at the opposite ends of the spectrum, both require the graciousness of humility. Mom understood how sports teach you to deal with the bumps and bruises in daily life.

Mom and Ben Press must have dedicated half the tennis courts in San Diego together, playing exhibitions long after her competitive career ended.

"I knew the public really wanted Maureen, but I was always flattered to be asked along," Ben said. "Actually, we only lost one doubles tournament together—that's my claim to fame. Always chose good partners, I say!

"I only saw her lose a few times—mainly because she didn't lose often! I was there when Beverly Blake Baker beat her one time. Maureen made no excuses. She was a gracious loser. Her attitude, in my opinion, was that a lot of people are poor losers—but there is nothing worse than a poor winner. Maureen never treated an opponent as an underling. Never made an excuse when she lost. She'd smile and tell the press, 'I was beaten by a better player today.' She was very gracious, very loving both in winning and losing."

What a grand tribute!

You're going to lose in life at some point. You're going to have some hard knocks. And, sometimes, you're going to win. But you have to learn how to be a gracious winner and loser. What Mom tried to instill in Brenda and me is that sports should teach you how to do both.

In the end, competition is one of the primary vehicles used to teach us an extraordinarily powerful lesson—and this may have been the real reason Mom was such a strong proponent of it:

"Sometimes, after very hard tennis matches," she once told a reporter, "I would find myself riding a crest of false satisfaction or, having lost, would be in the very lowest of spirits. But, after such a moment had passed, I would realize in reflecting, that everything we do is merely a part of God's plan and that victory or defeat is but a carrying out of His will. In this belief, I found a very valuable stabilizer.

"It is very easy in moments of glory to overlook the Divine Hand which guides us. The human element of self-satisfaction is always near and we sometimes tend to forget that, at a crucial point in a match, there was somehow an inner strength that allowed us to do the right thing at the right time.

"If we forget this for too long a period, it seems that a slight disappointment always comes about which brings us quickly back to an even train of thought."

Mom clearly recognized the source of her talents.

There is a funny article from *Parade* magazine in 1953—the height of Mom's popularity—"I'm No Swell-Head!" where the reporter rebuts allegations in an (unnamed) New York newspaper that success had gone to Little Mo's head.

Mom is in rare form in her closing statement:

I've gotten a lot of breaks through tennis—American tennis. I've traveled the world, met millions of people, and had a fine time. If it weren't for American coaches, I wouldn't be able to hold a racket. The American public encouraged me to play.

Swell-headed? Heavens, what have I got to be swell-headed about? I'm just an average American girl, who happens to have a talent for tennis the way other girls have a talent for music or dancing. I like to collect phonograph records almost as much as tennis records.

I'm not going to be a tennis player all my life. I look forward to getting married and settling down.

You can't have any fun out of life being a stuffed shirt. Having friends is a lot more important than getting your name in headlines. I hope that no one *really* believes those charges.

If I ever *do* become swell-headed, I hope somebody will knock it out of me—QUICK!

Parade interviewed other top American tennis players including Gardner Mulloy, Billy Talbert and Vic Seixas, all of whom agreed with the magazine's assessment that Little Mo was no prima donna. But the most interesting quote came from Mrs. Hazel Wightman, donor of the famed Wightman Cup:

She's one of the sweetest and the most natural eighteen-year-olds I know. I have fifteen girl players staying at my house including Maureen, Doris Hart, and Shirley Fry. They all like her. Gosh, even at dinnertime, she's the first to help. She's shy, but what poise!

To stay at the top, you have to continue to do the things that got you to the top in the first place. But once you start believing that you're the best—and that you'll always be the best—your downward slide is assured.

They called Mom "Little Miss Poker Face," not because she liked cards, but because she maintained the same demeanor whether winning or losing. She didn't bang her racket on the court, shout obscenities or question the linesman when she lost a point or a match.

Amazingly, during the last year of her career, she never lost a singles match in competitive play. And yet she treated each hopelessly overmatched opponent with dignity and respect—before, during, and after each match.

She repeatedly told me that competitors can choose between two approaches when facing an opponent: they either are afraid to lose or they want to win.

The psychology of both these two mindsets is focused on winning—but produces widely varying results. If players walk on the court afraid to lose, the results will become a self-fulfilled prophecy—they will lose. They will play tentatively and fearfully. Fear is the single most devastating emotion. It paralyzes any forward movement, dulls mental quickness, and suppresses risk taking. A fearful player cannot produce the big shots when they are needed.

Conversely, Mom always walked on the court wanting to win. In this psychological state, her confidence, alertness and focus soared. There was no lingering fear that would inhibit her play.

Since then, I have found those principles useful both personally and professionally. Fear holds me back. But desiring success is liberating and compels me forward with creativity, independent thinking and passion.

Mom's philosophy was to use the energy of a loss to promote winning. Not winning at any cost, mind you, but as part of a continued, life-long pursuit of excellence. As writer Ellen Langer says, "There are no failures, only ineffective solutions."

Mom once told me about a sign that hung over the doors at Wimbledon. It's a quote from Rudyard Kipling:

> *"If you can meet with Triumph and Disaster*
> *And treat those two impostors just the same."*

Humility and graciousness—winners and losers alike are victors with these attributes.

10

Lesson Seven

God Is Good!

Chris was ten years old when he died of cancer. He was an amazing young man. Chris had been one of our Wipe out Kids' Cancer ambassadors and we treasured our friendship with him and his family. Bob still carries Chris's picture in his briefcase. Bob and I went to see Chris in the hospital the day before he died. Bob had had a cold when I visited Chris at his home a month earlier, so he had been prevented from seeing Chris at that time. In the hospital, facing death, Chris was so concerned about Bob's health. He weakly asked, "How are you feeling? Are you over your cold? I am so sorry you were sick. You are so kind to take time to visit me. Thank you so much for coming here today."

His appreciation for our visit, his focus on us rather than himself truly overwhelmed Bob and me. We will never forget it.

This was from a child who would be dead in less than twenty-four hours.

At Chris's funeral, his father Rick got up to speak. As Rick stood there, looking over the standing-room-only group of mourners, trembling slightly, he began his comments with three powerful words, "God is good!"

In less than ten minutes, this man was about to bury his beloved son whom he adored, and yet he could still say, "God is good!"

I was shaken momentarily. How could he possibly say something like that while facing the single most devastating situation of his life? *How?*

Rick continued, only now he had the entire congregation's full attention:

"God was good to give me the privilege of fathering, loving, and nurturing Chris."

Then he went on to say that his son was a brief gift from our Heavenly Father and was returning for his homecoming. Rick said that Chris had taught him so many things in his short ten years. Chris was a blessing and to feel anything other than gratitude for God's precious gift would be unthinkable.

What Rick was sharing with the mourners assembled, Hebrews 11:1 calls "faith:"

"Now faith is being sure of what we hope for, and certain of what we do not see."

With that faith, Rick knew that Chris was now alive and present in the courts of our Creator, restored and filled with joy. Rick knew that God had not forgotten Chris or his family. God had, in Chris's illness, loved Chris just as much then as the day Chris was conceived. Rick knew that God had loved his family enough to give them a brave, wise, and mature-beyond-his-years son who had dramatically impacted each family member with his strength of character and humility. Rick knew that Chris was a gift. He knew all of this in faith.

However, Rick still missed Chris just as I still missed Mom. The hurt never goes away entirely. He and I talked about our losses—his son, my mother. But, in faith, our focus was different. We put our trust in God, no matter how numbing or agonizing our circumstances.

Like Rick, at times I would cry out, "God, I don't understand." And the tears would flow down my cheeks. But instead of putting a period after that phrase, I would insert a comma and say, "but God, I trust you."

That was where my life had changed. It had changed at the crossroads where my circumstances met my faith. It was at that place that my trust was now fully placed in God. Despite what was seen or what was unseen, I had full assurance that God had my best interest in mind. Rick knew that, too, even when his circumstances seemed to betray him.

Faith was the insertion of that simple comma and phrase—"but God, I trust you"—in my internal monologues. God hadn't abandoned our family. God didn't love our family less. God wasn't even mad at me. My view of God had changed. God had not changed—my heart had changed.

A few years ago, I saw a comic strip that amused me. The first frame of this comic strip featured a picture of an egg. The second frame had a picture of a crack in that egg, just a little crack. In the third frame, the head of a little chick popped out of the egg. In the fourth frame, the little chick looked to the left. In the fifth frame, the little chick looked to the right. In the sixth frame, the little chick looked ahead. And, in the final frame, that little chick grabbed the egg shell and jammed it back over his head!

That poor little chick was no different from me up to a point in my life. As the little chick surveyed his circumstances to the left, to the right, and straight ahead, they seemed quite overwhelming. The truth is—our circumstances can rob us of our joy when we look too closely. Retreat is about the only thing that seems feasible. But, whereas that little chick looked all around him, he forgot to look *up*. If we focus on God and not on our circumstances, we know that God has a plan and a purpose for us despite what we see in our circumstances. And understanding God's love for us transforms us—inside and out. It literally changes our hearts.

Elisabeth Kubler-Ross has done a number of studies that show that children with cancer can typically be more mature than healthy kids. I have experienced this through what I have observed with our ambassadors. Time and time

again, as I am in their presence, I am awed by their maturity
and sensitivity to the things around them.

I met a young boy named Trey when he was twelve. He
had a rare form of bone cancer and the doctors told his family that if they amputated his leg, they had a chance of arrest-
ing the cancer. If not, then he would surely die.

His parents didn't want to make that decision for him,
so they had Trey make it. He chose amputation.

Three days after his surgery, I had the privilege of
meeting Trey. Within minutes, we were fast friends.

As I sat on his hospital bed and we were cutting up like
old buddies, I said, "Trey, how do you feel after making such
a big decision? Are you okay with that?"

He looked at me very seriously and said, "Cindy, it was
an easy decision. It was my life or my leg." Then he started
joking around again.

But suddenly, Trey's mood changed and I could tell
that he wanted to make sure I understood. He became very
serious. Trey drew his face very close to mine and said very
emphatically, "Cindy, after all, it's *only* a leg."

No pouting, no complaining, no anger. Just a matter-
of-fact statement. Certainly no resentment or rage towards
God. On the contrary, Trey was grateful to God that he had
been saved. Once Trey got home and had time to heal, he
was out running, playing soccer, and enjoying the life of a
teenager. God is good!

Tara was a precious ambassador with Wipe Out Kids'
Cancer who shared God's goodness with all who knew and
loved her. Tara was thirteen when she died, a little Dresden
doll with glowing porcelain skin. Oh, she was so beautiful. I
was very close to Tara and her family.

After the funeral, Tara's mother called me. She said,
"Cindy, Tara made the most unusual request. Tara asked me
never to forget her. And she wanted me to call you and to ask
you never to forget her, too."

At first I thought that this was a bit of an unusual request
from a person of Tara's age. But as I got to thinking about it,

I realized how wise Tara was. Because, in the human perspective, that happens.

American journalist and politician Horace Greeley once wrote, "Fame is a vapor, popularity is an accident, riches take wings." What he was saying, and what Tara realized, is that life is temporary. We can be on top today, but our circumstances may quickly reverse. And people have very short memories.

We can be assured that God never forgets us.

God is good! That same God who gave Tara and Chris to their families, gave Mom to me. God was not on vacation when Mom breathed her last breath. The Creator who gave her life was there. God was not looking elsewhere when Chris and Tara died. God was there. God did not turn His back when Trey's leg was amputated or when Linda Kearbey drove down that Missouri highway. God was there. God didn't go to sleep when Allen Bolden checked out that night from his lifeguard duty. God was there.

God is good! He gave me a Mom for twelve years, a mom who could still inspire me by her example more than thirty years later.

God does not forget you or me. All of humanity is a living soul of significance because God breathed His breath into us and made us into His image.

God is good!

To this day, so many people can still see God through Mom, through all of her professional and personal talents. Mom did not earn her talents; she did not earn her tremendous giftedness. These were God-given gifts.

You could see God at work in Mom. She worked hard all her career, but she had basic, fundamental talents—like her tenacity, like her determination, like her desire to succeed, like her raw abilities. Those were God-given. I practiced a whole lot during my tennis career, but no matter how hard I worked, no matter if I practiced the same hours that Mom practiced, I would still never be as good as Mom. Because what she had, that indefinable gift, was a gift from God.

And Mom is with God in glory now.

God was with Mom when she won Wimbledon three times just as much as when she was dying of cancer. God was with our family before she got sick and when we buried her. God is *always* there.

The second half of Hebrews 13:5 says, ". . . God has said, never will I leave you, never will I forsake you." God is there. God grieves when we grieve, God rejoices when we rejoice—just as we grieve when our children are sad, just as we rejoice when our children are happy.

The old hymn "Our Great Savior" by J. Wilbur Chapman and Rowland J. Pritchard is a beautiful testament to the comfort and peace we can find in our Lord and Savior Jesus Christ. The third verse is particularly powerful:

"Jesus! What a Help in sorrow! While the billows o'er me roll, even when my heart is breaking, He, my Comfort, helps my soul. Hallelujah! What a Savior! Hallelujah! What a Friend! Saving, helping, keeping, loving, He is with me to the end."

God doesn't just love me, God loves me with abandon.

Even when my world is caving in.

Our little William loves the circus. And when we go, we typically buy him a red balloon. William loves red balloons. But the inevitable always happens—the balloon pops. Bob is very much a handyman—he can fix anything. When anything breaks around our home, William always shouts, "Let's get Daddy to fix it! Daddy can fix anything, Mommy!" But no matter how hard Bob would try, he could not fix the flattened pile of red rubber that was once William's balloon. No matter how many times William would automatically reach out to Bob and say, "Fix it, Daddy! Please fix it!," Bob would not be able to get that burst balloon to inflate again.

But there is another Father whom we can go to with our pile of brokenness—our shattered dreams, weary souls, fragile hearts, and deep discouragement. And we can reach out to this Father with our pile of rubble and say, "Fix it, Daddy! Please fix it!" This Father can reconcile that which was lost and make whole that which was broken. He can love the unlovable and make clean what was unclean.

I see how good God is to have given me a Mom like He did even though she was taken at thirty-four, even though I was a motherless child at twelve. For the fact that I got such a great mom, I give all the credit to God.

And yet we still resist God's love.

Martin Luther tells a wonderful story from his childhood. At age 10, he and another friend were Christmas caroling door to door when one door flew open and a large man appeared in the doorway holding a club in one hand and a lamp in the other.

Martin and his friend fled shrieking down the street, the man in hot pursuit, all the while shouting "Stop, stop!" Finally, they inadvertently turned into a dead-end alley and waited, quaking in fear, for the man with the club to arrive. But when the man turned the corner, they saw that he actually had a big sausage that he'd been trying to give to them.

Years later, Luther wrote about this incident. He said that all of his life he'd been led to believe that God was someone who had a big club who spent His time shouting "Stop, stop!" But in truth, God was a loving Creator who only wanted to give Luther the things he wanted.

God is good!

God loves me too much to let me be separated from Him and be comfortable.

As God loved my mom, so my mom loved me. She never asked me for anything in return. All she wanted was that I accept that love. More than thirty years later, I still feel that unconditional love. Her life was a living, breathing parable to me. In those few, short years, she taught me so much. I'm thankful every day for the opportunity, for the time, I had with her.

An entry from my journal on June 21, 1976, Mom's death anniversary, sums up both the sadness I felt in Mom's loss and the depth of gratitude I felt in God's goodness:

> Oh Mom, PLEASE know that I think you were and always will be, the BEST mother . . . How many times I wish you were with me, helping me make decisions, deciding what to wear, how to deal with the guys. I MISS

you so. I know my tears just show how selfish I am—I
know God is good to you—you feel no pain in
heaven—and PLEASE know that I am happiest for that.
It totally broke my heart to hear you cry out loud in pain.
How I miss you! . . . I know God is good and does everything for a reason—as hidden as it may be at the time . . .

Then, this journal entry ends in a prayer:

Dear Lord,
I pray you will look over Mom in Heaven . . . I thank you,
dear Lord, for letting me be blessed with her as a
mother—I feel so fortunate . . . I know there was a reason
for her loss and I really do trust in you . . . Oh Lord, most
importantly, I thank you for letting me be blessed with
mom—she is such a model of perfection. I just pray I can
be half as wonderful as her when I get older. Lord, my
tears are only testimony of the great love, devotion, and
admiration I had, and always will have, of Mom. God
bless that wonderful individual, that gallant lady,
Maureen Connolly Brinker, wife, mother, champion.
Amen

Today, more than ever, I know this one eternal truth:

God is good!

Appendix A
Little Mo's Record

Mom's accomplishments look even more incredible when they are placed in chronological order. She dominated tennis like few champions have dominated any sport in history.

What was her greatest accomplishment? I suspect Mom, with her typically humble spirit, would have cited her marriage to Dad or raising a couple of normal (well, reasonably normal!), kids.

But Nancy Jeffett, who knew her so well, did offer a rare insight into the heart of a champion. Mom was, after all, a young girl, a teenager, winning those championships. And Nancy believes that at least one of the highlights of Mom's career came the night following her third Wimbledon championship in 1954:

In the past at Wimbledon, the Wimbledon Ball was held the final night. It was a long-standing tradition that the men's and women's champions danced a dance together. Back then, Maureen's favorite song was Nat King Cole's 'Unforgettable.' I was there, and I'll never forget the look on her face when the men's champion, Jaroslav Drobny, asked her to dance, just as the opening strains of 'Unforgettable' sounded.

In retrospect, it was a fairy-tale ending to her career. It was only a few weeks after Wimbledon that year that she had the terrible horseback riding accident. But nothing ever dimmed her enthusiasm, her will to live or that strong sense of joy that surrounded her.

Mom was unforgettable.

A very abbreviated overview of her otherwise short, but spectacular, tennis career is breathtaking. Mom started playing tennis in 1944, the year she turned ten, and was forced to abdicate her reign over women's tennis in 1954, the year she turned twenty, because of a serious horseback riding accident. She was a member of the U.S. Wightman Cup Team from 1951–1954, winning all nine of her matches. In fact, she did not lose a singles match the last year of her competitive career. I have encapsulated her most prominent achievements:

1944   Began playing tennis
1947   Ranked number 2 by Southern California Tennis Association for girls under 15 years old
1948   Southern California 18-year-old Division Champion
1950   National Jr. (18 and under) Girls' Singles Champion
       National Jr. (18 and under) Girls' Doubles Champion
       Ranked Number 1 Junior Girl by United States Lawn Tennis Association
       Ranked Number 10 in USLTA Women's Division
1951   U. S. Open Women's Singles Champion
       Member of U.S. Wightman Cup Team
       Ranked Number 1 in USLTA Women's Division
       Voted "Woman Athlete of the Year" by Associated Press
1952   Wimbledon Women's Singles Champion
       U. S. Open Women's Singles Champion
       Ireland Singles Champion
       Member of U.S. Wightman Cup Team
       Ranked Number 1 in USLTA Women's Division
       Ranked Number 1 in the World
       Voted "Woman Athlete of the Year" by Associated Press for the second consecutive year
1953   Australian Singles and Doubles Champion
       French Singles Champion
       Wimbledon Women's Singles Champion
       U. S. Open Women's Singles Champion
       (First and youngest woman to date to win Grand Slam)
       U.S. Clay Court Champion
       Member of U.S. Wightman Cup Team
       Ranked Number 1 in USLTA Women's Division
       Ranked Number 1 in the World
       Voted "Woman Athlete of the Year" by Associated Press for the third consecutive year
1954   Wimbledon Singles Champion
       French Singles and Mixed Doubles Champion
       U.S. Clay Court Singles and Doubles Champion
       Ireland Singles Champion
       Italian Singles and Mixed Doubles Champion
       Member of U.S. Wightman Cup Team
       (Mom did not receive a national or world ranking in 1954 because of her July horseback riding accident, which prevented her from competing the rest of the year.)
1968   Elected to the International Tennis Hall of Fame

Appendix B
The Maureen Connolly Brinker Tennis Foundation

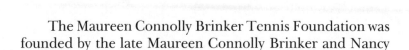

The Maureen Connolly Brinker Tennis Foundation was founded by the late Maureen Connolly Brinker and Nancy Jeffett in 1968.

Mrs. Jeffett, with fellow directors Brenda Brinker Bottum, Norman Brinker, Elizabeth Jeffett Norman, Cindy Brinker Simmons, and Bob Taylor, a dedicated advisory board and Executive Director Carol Weyman, leads the foundation in its continuing and expanding efforts to strengthen girls', boys' and women's tennis. Specifically, the foundation provides the benefits of tennis to increasing numbers of youngsters all over the world. The success of the Maureen Connolly Brinker Tennis Foundation has traveled throughout the United States with tournaments and programs.

Some of the many tournaments and programs supported and sponsored by the Maureen Connolly Brinker Tennis Foundation include:

Maureen Connolly Cup (ladies 55 and over)
ITF Connolly Continental Cup (girls 18 and under for all nations)
Maureen Connolly Challenge Trophy (U.S. vs. Great Britain for girls 19 and under)
Maureen Connolly Brinker Cup (U.S. vs. Australia for girls 14, 16 and 18)
MCB Girls' 14 National Championships (girls 14 and under)
"Little Mo" (nationwide program for boys and girls 8, 9, 10, 11 and under)
MCB Cotton Bowl Classic
Dallas National Junior Tennis League (inner-city youth program)
USTA Boys' 18 Indoors—Art Foust Award

USTA Girls' 18 Nationals—Outstanding Junior Girl Award
The Dallas Tennis Association (schools program, wheelchair tennis,
        junior excellence, and McKinley Cup)
Tennis Competitors of Dallas (ladies league for over 5,000 members)
Metroplex Tennis League (businesswomen's league for 1,500 members)
MCB Tennis Foundation in Wichita, Kansas
Sportsmanship awards and travel grants
Virginia Slims of Dallas professional women's tennis tournament
        (1970–1989)

For more information about the Maureen Connolly Brinker
Tennis Foundation, please call (214) 352-7978 or e-mail:
Cartennis@aol.com.